MULTICULTURAL EDUCATION SERIES

James A. Banks, Series Editor

Multicultural Strategies for Education and Social Change

CARRIERS OF THE TORCH
IN THE UNITED STATES AND SOUTH AFRICA

Arnetha F. Ball

Foreword by Shirley Brice Heath

Teachers College, Columbia University
New York and London

Published by Teachers College Press, 1234 Amsterdam Avenue, New York, NY 10027

Library of Congress Cataloging-in-Publication Data

Ball, Arnetha F., 1950–
   Multicultural strategies for education and social change : carriers of the torch in the United States and South Africa / Arnetha F. Ball.
     p. cm. — (Multicultural education series)
   Includes bibliographical references and index.
   ISBN 0-8077-4670-3 (cloth : alk. paper)—ISBN 0-8077-4669-X (pbk. : alk. paper)
   1. Teachers—Training of—Cross-cultural studies. 2. Teachers—Training of—United States. 3. Teachers—Training of—South Africa. 4. Social change—United States. 5. Social change—South Africa. I. Title. II. Multicultural education series (New York, N.Y.)

   LB1707.B35 2006
   370.117—dc22

                             2005055931

ISBN-13:   ISBN-10:
978-0-8077-4669-1 (paper)   0-8077-4669-X (paper)
978-0-8077-4670-7 (cloth)   0-8077-4670-3 (cloth)

Printed on acid-free paper
Manufactured in the United States of America

13 12 11 10 09 08 07 06   8 7 6 5 4 3 2 1

In memory of
Madoda Ntilashe,
a very powerful teacher and advocate for social change
who touched the lives of many students,
and
to my mother,
Mildred Hayes Mathews,
who instilled and nurtured in me
a sense of efficacy and advocacy

Hold high the torch . . .
'Tis yours to keep it burning bright,
Yours to pass on when others need more light;
For there are other feet that we must guide,
And those who go marching by our side,
Their eyes are watching every tear and smile,
And efforts which we think are not worthwhile,
Are sometimes just the very helps they need,
Actions to which their souls would give most heed,
So that in turn they'll hold it high, and say,
"I watched someone else carry it in this way."
. . . Hold high the torch of beauty, truth, and love . . .
"Ye are the light of the world.
Go! . . . Shine for me."

—Dorothy M. Howard

Contents

Series Foreword

THE NATION'S DEEPENING ethnic texture, interracial tension, and conflict and the increasing percentage of students who speak a first language other than English make multicultural education imperative in the 21st century. The U.S. Census Bureau (2000) estimates that people of color made up 28% of the nation's population in 2000 and predicts that they will make up 38% in 2025 and 50% in 2050 (El Nasser, 2004).

American classrooms are experiencing the largest influx of immigrant students since the beginning of the 20th century. About a million immigrants are making the United States their home each year (Martin & Midgley, 1999). More than 7.5 million legal immigrants settled in the United States between 1991 and 1998, most of them from nations in Latin America and Asia (Riche, 2000) and a significant number from the West Indies and Africa. A large but undetermined number of undocumented immigrants also enter the United States each year. The influence of an increasingly ethnically diverse population on the nation's schools, colleges, and universities is and will continue to be enormous.

Forty percent of the students enrolled in the nation's schools in 2001 were students of color. This percentage is increasing each year, primarily because of the growth in the percentage of Latino students (Martinez & Curry, 1999). In some of the nation's largest cities and greater metropolitan areas, such as Chicago; Los Angeles; Washington, DC; New York; Seattle; and San Francisco, at least half of the public school students are students of color. During the 1998–1999 school year, students of color made up 63.1% of the student population in the public schools of California, the nation's largest state (California State Department of Education, 2000).

Language and religious diversity are also increasing among the nation's student population. In 2000, about 20% of the school-age population spoke a language at home other than English (U.S. Census Bureau, 2000). Harvard professor Diana L. Eck (2001) calls the United States the "most religiously diverse nation on earth" (p. 4). Islam is now the fastest-growing religion in the United States. Most teachers currently in the classroom and in teacher education programs are likely to work with students from a wide range of ethnic, racial, language, and religious groups during their careers. This is true for both inner-city and suburban teachers.

An important goal of multicultural education is to improve race relations and to help all students acquire the knowledge, attitudes, and skills
needed for participation in cross-cultural interactions and in personal, social, and civic action that will help make our nation more democratic and
just. Multicultural education is consequently as important for middle-class
White suburban students as it is for students of color who live in the inner
city. Multicultural education fosters the public good and the overarching goals
of the commonwealth.

The major purpose of the Multicultural Education Series is to provide
preservice educators, practicing educators, graduate students, scholars, and
policy makers with an interrelated and comprehensive set of books that sum-
marizes and analyzes important research, theory, and practice related to the
education of different ethnic, racial, cultural, and language groups in
the United States and the education of mainstream students about diversity.
The books in the series provide research, theoretical, and practical knowledge about the behaviors and learning characteristics of students of color,
language-minority students, and low-income students. They also provide
knowledge about ways to improve academic achievement and race relations
in educational settings.

The definition of multicultural education in the *Handbook of Research
on Multicultural Education* (Banks & Banks, 2004) is used in the series:
Multicultural education is "*a field of study designed to increase educational
equity for all students that incorporates, for this purpose, content, concepts,
principles, theories, and paradigms from history, the social and behavioral
sciences, and particularly from ethnic studies and women's studies*" (p. xii).
In the series, as in the *Handbook*, multicultural education is considered a
"metadiscipline."

The dimensions of multicultural education, developed by Banks (2004b)
and described in the *Handbook of Research on Multicultural Education*,
provide the conceptual framework for the development of the books in the
series. They are *content integration, the knowledge construction process,
prejudice reduction, an equity pedagogy,* and *an empowering school culture
and social structure.* To implement multicultural education effectively,
teachers and administrators must attend to each of the five dimensions of
multicultural education. They should use content from diverse groups when
teaching concepts and skills; help students to understand how knowledge in
the various disciplines is constructed; help students to develop positive intergroup attitudes and behaviors; and modify their teaching strategies so that
students from different racial, cultural, language, and social-class groups will
experience equal educational opportunities. The total environment and culture of the school must also be transformed so that students from diverse
groups will experience equal status in the culture and life of the school.

Although the five dimensions of multicultural education are highly interrelated, each requires deliberate attention and focus. Each book in the series focuses on one or more of the dimensions, although each book deals with all of them to some extent because of the highly interrelated characteristics of the dimensions.

The education of students from diverse racial, ethnic, cultural, language, and religious groups is a problem that challenges educators on every continent (Banks, 2004a). The diversity in former colonial nations such as the United States, Canada, Australia, and South Africa intensified when the European colonizers of these lands disrupted native cultures, eradicated aboriginal languages and institutions, and imposed European values and folkways and a racial caste system that codified White supremacy. The system of chattel slavery that was established in the Caribbean, the United States, and Brazil reinforced and institutionalized White supremacy and left a powerful and pernicious legacy of racialization, which these nations have yet to overcome. Racialization affects educators and students in these nations in significant ways today, as this informative book by Arnetha Ball makes clear.

An important consequence of European colonization in the 16th and 17th centuries is the flow of immigrants from former colonies who have settled in Europe since World War II seeking economic, political, and educational opportunities. These immigrant populations have significantly changed the racial, ethnic, linguistic, and religious texture of European nations such as England, France, and The Netherlands. The diversity brought to Europe by immigrants from its former colonies has also increased racial, ethnic, and religious tension and conflict. The establishment of a policy by the French government that bans from public schools the wearing of religious symbols such as the headscarf worn by Muslim girls is a desperate attempt by a nation with a strong assimilationist history and ideology to deal with religious expression in the public sphere. As worldwide immigration increases diversity on every continent, nation-states are searching for ways to balance unity and diversity (Banks et al., 2005).

Ethnic and religious strife, tension, and violence are intense in many regions of the globe. World events underscore the need for schools to help reduce ethnic tension and create civic and just communities; they also reveal the global challenge of preparing teachers for diversity, the subject of this timely book. The London subway and bus bombings that killed at least 56 people and injured more than 700 on July 7, 2005, deepened ethnic and religious tension and Islamophobia in Europe after the police announced that the suspected perpetuators were Muslim suicide bombers. Negative feelings about Muslims in Europe had already increased after Moroccans—who were North African Arabs—bombed four commuter trains in Madrid, Spain, killing 191 people, on March 11, 2004. Ethnic and religious strife in Europe influences intergroup relations in the schools in significant and complex ways and presents new challenges for educating teachers for multicultural classrooms and schools, the focus of this book.

Of the former European colonies, the United States and South Africa have perhaps the deepest and most intransigent legacy of institutionalized racism and apartheid. This has powerful effects on the education of Black and White students in both nations, as Ball documents in this significant, instructive, and hopeful book. The racialization legacy in the United States and South Africa also affects the knowledge, attitudes, beliefs, and dispositions of teachers in both nations.

Ball, drawing on a decade of teacher education work in the two countries, describes how the lives and work of teachers can enrich the theory and practice of teacher education. In this book, both visionary and practical, she also reveals how her teacher education courses—which used writing as pedagogy—helped teachers to develop commitment and agency and become transformative educators who are "carriers of the torch."

We are living in troubled and challenging times for teacher education (Cochran-Smith, 2004). The standardization movement—which was given new life and intensified by the passage of the No Child Left Behind Act in 2001—often defines knowledge acquisition as the mastery of measurable facts and views teachers as technicians who should follow a script. It is thus refreshing and empowering to hear a voice such as Arnetha Ball's articulate a complex and visionary view of teaching and learning. Teacher education in both the United States and South Africa will be greatly enriched if her voice is heard and heeded.

James A. Banks
Series Editor

REFERENCES

Banks, J. A. (Ed.). (2004a). *Diversity and citizenship education: Global perspectives*. San Francisco: Jossey-Bass.

Banks, J. A. (2004b). Multicultural education: Historical development, dimensions, and practice. In J. A. Banks & C. A. M. Banks (Eds.), *Handbook of research on multicultural education* (2nd ed., pp. 3–29). San Francisco: Jossey-Bass.

Banks, J. A., & Banks, C. A. M. (Eds.). (2004). *Handbook of research on multicultural education* (2nd ed.). San Francisco: Jossey-Bass.

Banks, J. A., Banks, C. A. M., Cortés, C. E., Hahn, C. L., Merryfield, M. M., Moodley, K. A., Murphy-Shigematsu, S., Osler, A., Park, C., & Parker, W. C. (2005). *Democracy and diversity: Principles and concepts for educating citizens in a global age*. Seattle: Center for Multicultural Education, University of Washington.

California State Department of Education. (2000). http://data1.cde.ca.gov/dataquest.

Cochran-Smith, M. (2004). *Walking the road: Essays on race, diversity, and social justice in teacher education.* New York: Teachers College Press.

Eck, D. L. (2001). *A new religious America: How a "Christian country" has become the world's most religiously diverse nation.* New York: HarperSanFrancisco.

El Nasser, H. (2004, March 18). Census projects growing diversity: By 2050: Population burst, societal shifts. *USA Today*, p. 1A.

Martin, P., & Midgley, E. (1999). Immigration to the United States. *Population Bulletin*, 54(2), 1–44. Washington, DC: Population Reference Bureau.

Martinez, G. M., & Curry, A. E. (1999, September). *Current population reports: School enrollment—social and economic characteristics of students.* (Update). Washington, DC: U.S. Census Bureau.

Riche, M. F. (2000). America's diversity and growth: Signposts for the 21st century. *Population Bulletin*, 55(2), 1–43. Washington, DC: Population Reference Bureau.

United States Census Bureau (2000). *Statistical abstract of the United States* (120th edition). Washington, DC: U.S. Government Printing Office.

Foreword

O N THE WALL of my study hangs a large black-and-white photograph (reproduced on the cover of this book) of a young girl from Soweto whose chair is drawn close to a boarded-up window. Through a long thin crack in the boards, a sliver of light slips into the darkened room. The girl's expression is intent, her hands tightly holding a book in front of her at a high slant so as to catch the available light on the book's pages.

Clive Gray, a photographer and medical researcher, took the photograph in the 1980s in Soweto. Each week, his wife, Heather Brookes, an educator, left their comfortable White neighborhood and went to Soweto to read, talk, and listen to children eager to learn but kept from schools because of the township violence. Heather and Clive had joined with others from White enclaves in Johannesburg and other cities and towns throughout South Africa who had become "teachers" in the face of critical need. Those who braved the dangers of entering townships in those years did so in an effort to find their own ways to fill the gaping educational void created during the township violence of the 1980s. In doing so, they came face to face with the many complexities of reaching across political and historical borders as well as cultural and self-identity barriers. But they did so without crossing into the official status of "teacher" or the institution of "school."

In the 1980s, when most schools in townships around Johannesburg closed, learning, reading, and studying were forbidden fruits of education. Children sought out church halls, the back rooms of tiny shops, and even the backyards of shacks scattered through the townships. There those who were lucky found emissaries who brought books, commitment, and English-dominant conversation. When the violence became chaotically severe and more random, entry to the townships by Whites from Johannesburg became impossible, but the books and will of the children remained. Some of what they had learned slipped into popular theater, songs, and spontaneous performances in the townships. By 1994, with the release of Nelson Mandela and the possibility of elections, the hopes of many children remained high for a renewal of the learning opportunities they had had in the furtive and sporadic volunteer "schooling" of the 1980s.

Shortly after Mandela was elected president, Arnetha Ball went to South Africa in an effort to understand what would happen as teachers, teaching, and schooling in the townships were joined together in local, regional, and national institutions of education. The nation undertook with dedication the goal of rebuilding, reopening, and stabilizing schools that would be free of the cultural, class, and spatial barriers that had been imposed under apartheid.

Ball brought to South Africa her background of action, reflection, and research on the skills, attitudes, and philosophies of teachers working in the United States. Differences and similarities between teacher education in South Africa and in the United States challenged her, as they would anyone coming to South Africa from other contexts of struggle against racism, poverty, violence, and political repression. This volume lays out many of those challenges while also demonstrating some parallels and insurmountable differences.

In this Foreword, I reflect on possible directions ahead for the persistence of habits as well as the twists and turns of change that this comparative study of teacher education suggests. These reflections come from my own experiences as a linguistic anthropologist participating in and observing learning environments of subordinated populations in South Africa and the United States, as well as Latin American and European nations. The central lens through which I cast these comments is that of adult learning. Teacher education calls on adults to change habits, attitudes, and resistant institutions at a time when these adults face tough demands in their personal lives. To think, instruct, and judge in new ways in a climate of rapid, often random, and even violent change is the challenge teachers in both South Africa and the United States face.

Education policies and practices generally direct themselves to student learning; to give equal attention to teachers as learners is rare. Yet, ultimately, lasting effects of any learning environment—whether school, family, religious organization, or workplace—depend on the reciprocal learning of those who take on the role of "teacher" and those given a "student" role.

We are born with the ability to learn throughout life. Yet nations that are historically dependent on formal education socialize citizens into the view that certain contexts—those labeled as *school, training,* or *education*—must take center stage to prepare citizens and workers. Casting ahead to what learners will do in the future once they have learned in school discourages the idea that students and teachers have ongoing reciprocal responsibilities for learning together. This volume amply illustrates how Ball learned with her students as they also learned.

This pattern of teacher and student learning together helps ensure retention of skills and information and instills respect for what students as well as teachers bring to any learning environment. Most learning throughout life goes on beyond the boundaries of formal education. Moreover, as we mature, the ways we forget, compare, gain, and assess new skills and knowledge become increasingly shaped by our perceived needs for our own learning.

In particular, attitudes toward the future, ours and that of family, job, community, nation, or even the world, determine degrees of commitment and applications of what we have gained in skills and knowledge. Respecting what others know, how they have learned, and what their experiences have given to a community or nation multiplies positive effects of situations in which teaching and learning go on simultaneously.

Herein lies a central issue of teacher education today in both the United States and South Africa. Most of those who enter teaching as their chosen profession bear strong influence from the years when entirely different worlds existed in separate schools (i.e., "Model C" in South Africa; "academic," "vocational," or "special" in the United States). Moreover, many would-be teachers chose to do their teacher training in higher education institutions close to their home, while the geographic locations of their own teaching careers could be very distant—culturally and physically. These academic, social, and geographic demarcations between location of training and that of teaching often amount to poor preparation for respecting student worlds and the history of communities and cultures they represent. Teachers often enter classrooms with their own narrow experience of race and class relations as well as their assumption that formal education must reflect the interests of capitalist expansion. These divisions between students and teachers receive reinforcement through differences in languages and language use, as well as regional identities and family allegiances. All these divisions endanger the possibilities of mutual respect and open communication.

South African writers have referred to the definitional power of these distinctions as "spatial madness." It is a well-known fact that urbanized Blacks in South Africa were severed from their rural origins and could lay no future claim to their "own" spaces. Dispossession still marks immigrants, migrant workers, and guestworkers in Europe, Latin America, and North America, just as it did many African Americans who left their homes in the South to move north after World War II and during the civil rights era. Family history of spatial dislocation plus entry into culturally and geographically distant places for learning and teaching generate defensiveness, fear, and barriers to learning. Many would-be teachers at urban universities and teacher training programs in South Africa come from either townships or rural areas, live in single rooms in run-down boarding houses, and in their daily classes meet little respect for their life experiences.

Spatial separations that ultimately bring dispossession inevitably coincide with culturally different ideas of property maintenance and time management. Those schooled in separate spaces come to hold very different values about seemingly subtle variations that can trigger strong reactions and intense judgments. For example, professional training in teaching builds upon fundamental attitudes about independence with regard to responsibility, respect for private property, and effective uses of one's time. These values in turn link to ideas about character, gender roles, and ambitions.

Teacher education programs tend to instill in teachers the idea that achievement is and "should be" based on independent learning acquired in line with the norms of educational institutions (especially those related to collaboration, honesty, and respect for hierarchies). Moreover, academic achievement is expected to be propelled by individual ambitions for the future roles of "good" citizen and "productive" worker. White, European-based ideas of gender undergird professional educators' training and perpetuate the view that educated young women will be able to enter the capitalist system without fear of violence or exploitation as sex objects.

Sadly, many of these values and expectations, as well as ideas linked to the belief that prosperity can ensure physical safety, fly in the face of current realities. At the most personal level, the threat of violence inhibits the movements, possibilities, and promises for all young women—especially in South Africa. Regardless of educational aspirations and instilled beliefs, women and the young can rarely overcome barriers that keep them distant from real independence, significant economic gains, and leadership in social reforms.

Key to deep-cutting alterations of teacher education in South Africa and the United States is the need for all adults to engage with these and other contradictions as well as the support of these elements by formal education. Teachers learn in their professional preparation to protect their role as teacher and to stand apart from the learning they urge their students to take up. Teacher training typically offers minimal guidance about ways to help students sustain and extend skills and knowledge or assess and alter institutional barriers. Teacher education programs and ongoing professional development programs shy away from encouraging or modeling risky self-exploration. The fact that "no answer" may be the only result of such inquiry runs counter to expected relationships between teacher and student.

But teacher education is not alone in sometimes seeming to be overwhelmed by the certainty of change in the face of the unknown and unpredictable. Consider a cultural institution long thought of as in the forefront of change in South Africa—theater, including poetry, song, and dance. Whether the origin of drama comes from the pen of South Africa's playwrights or spontaneously from village or township improvisations, the words and movements of theater have challenged what is and what has been. South African theater was introduced to the world stage through its powerful representations of the personal and political horrors inflicted under apartheid.

Since 1994, professional theater in South Africa has had to confront terrors that lie not in political tyranny but within the critical need to create faith, will, and an equitable course toward an undefined future. Theater and song now must be about learning to forgive and to face intergenerational and spatial chasms. Moreover, there is a need to question the efficacy of morality as well as the protective value of any given boundary. Some dramatic works also attempt to confront the paralyzing force of new fears linked to the random and rapid course of AIDS as killer. Traditional imperatives, including those of truth, loyalty, and developmental trajectories, now thrown violently into question, do not easily find their way into contemporary drama, poetry, or song. Thus religion as palliative, magic as imperative, and myth as rationale appear to be the most attractive supports on which some characters in current South African literature now rely. Some of these beliefs not only feed past divisions but also create new rationales for violence, such as those reflected in the view that sees child rape as a "cure" for AIDS. Worker theater has veered away from performance of a revolutionary autobiographical subject and now flounders—uncertain of its role in the wake of the narrowly beneficial and yet rampant force of multinational corporate influence in South Africa. Teacher education and theater both struggle to reflect and inspire continual learning.

Accuracy and truth are sometimes quite different things. Both come up against the difficult trick of recognizing the past as always a part of the present and, decidedly for the less powerful, a strong but unpredictable determinant of the meaning of the future. The implications of these statements for teacher education have to be set within the reality that during those years in which teachers are being professionally prepared, they simultaneously have to be seeking stability in human relationships. Ball's volume reflects in numerous ways the constant course of self-definition that teachers as professionals face even as they undergo role shifts and sometimes tumultuous changes within their intimate circles of family. To place oneself during these years (when one is generally between one's early 20s and late 40s) into deep interior examinations of truth and accuracy with regard to cultural, linguistic, gender, and spatial issues is to take inordinate risks. A well-known plot twist in one's life course is that the adolescent years are those in which risks are willingly taken on. Yet middle and later adulthood bring many "natural" uncertainties and challenges in the personal life course. Many teachers with whom Arnetha Ball worked in South Africa were first-time homeowners relocated from their townships to new communities. The hard psychological and financial work of such personal changes inevitably discourages risk-taking in one's professional life. Fatigue, time limits, and ease of doing things the familiar way overwhelm any urge to learn how to manage cultural, linguistic, and attitudinal differences in innovative reflective ways. Yet it is during middle and later adulthood that adults most need to learn, and to learn broadly, for the future benefit of their rapidly changing communities.

In 2005, actor and playwright John Kani brought his play *Nothing but the Truth* to the United States. The play centers on adult learning. Kani, an actor-writer who helped mold Athol Fugard's *Sizwe Banzi Is Dead* and *The Island* during the apartheid years, takes on truth, accuracy, and the relative degrees of wrongness or rightness that reside within silence, complacency, anger, and resentment. The play makes clear that older professionals (the lead is a librarian) find it natural and defensible to be most centrally focused on their own career advancement and personal needs. Thus one can find all sorts of reasons to resent and resist the values of a new system or the expectations of the culturally different, or even the young within one's own family. Novelist J. M. Coetzee, in *Disgrace*, brings us a similar story.

To succeed in enabling teachers to take themselves into the many challenges shaped by rapid cultural, political, and social changes will mean doing far more than this volume details. Yet the stories that Ball tells here of creative means of persuasion and thoughtful acceptance of cross-cutting practices inspired by learning theorists should do more than prod us to deeper thinking.

The history here of the decade from the mid-1990s to the middle of the first decade of the 21st century points to some new directions that will, no doubt, be shaped by the young people who enter the profession of teaching in the coming decade. Boundaries between schools and other learning environments will continue to fall or at least fade. Voices to challenge schools' traditional means of teaching and testing will grow louder and shriller. Employers in the global marketplace will increasingly assert their need for employees who think creatively, invent new approaches, and excel in anticipating problems, market demands, and product successes. Employers have moved beyond wanting workers who are mere repositories of skills and factual information that is rapidly becoming outdated. National educational systems, such as those of Singapore, England, and The Netherlands, are already building creative learning into the demands of teachers and students. The usual power relationships between teacher and student are being deeply challenged as young inventors, often in their teen years, displace established commercial processes and products, particularly in the software and media industries.

Such realities will increasingly mark learning across the life span and be ever more forcibly driven by capitalist urges and fears of competition from newly emerging international powers. Social categories, as well as institutional boundaries, formerly taken to be given and immutable, are already being viewed as interdependent and volatile. Local and global contexts of communication and commercialization now emphasize efforts to discover means that make learning consequential far beyond any individual or group currently in power.

These forces promise to push harder and harder against what teachers, students, and educational institutions have thought would remain certain or grounded. The direction ahead is surely indicated by philosopher Ludwig Wittgenstein's caution "If the true is what is grounded, then the ground is not true, nor yet false" (p. 28).

I have no idea what happened to the young girl from Soweto whose photograph hangs on the wall of my study. My fantasy is that her beginnings with books, learning, and lessons on the power of tiny openings of light have continued to have the transformative effects indicated in this volume's stories of teacher education. I like to imagine that today, in her late 20s, she is teaching, learning, and leading. I like to think that the tiny sliver of light in this photograph has become for the youth of the coming generation an open window, that she and fellow teachers and her students see there possibilities to cultivate and enrich the ground for new accuracies and future truths.

—Shirley Brice Heath

Preface

I AM GENERALLY a very happy and outgoing person and I think of myself as a pretty effective teacher, especially when working with young students from culturally and linguistically diverse backgrounds. On my university teacher education course evaluations, students have characterized me as "outgoing and knowledgeable, with a very engaging personality, and obviously passionate about her teaching." At one point in my career, however, I found that I was leaving my teacher education classroom feeling dejected and, in general, as if I were failing my students. You see, I entered the teacher education profession because of my concern about the deplorable conditions under which poor and underachieving students from diverse backgrounds are expected to learn in today's schools. Jonathan Kozol (1992) writes about these conditions, describing, for example, East St. Louis as "a repository for a nonwhite population that is now regarded as expendable. The *Post-Dispatch* describes it as 'America's Soweto'" ("Sewage Problems," 1989, p. 8). These Soweto-like conditions are found in the schools of East St. Louis, Harlem and the Bronx in New York City, Chicago, Jersey City, Compton, and San Antonio in the United States; and in Alexandria, Khayelitsha, Guguletu, Umlaze, and Umdane in South Africa, where students from poor families attend grossly underequipped, understaffed, and underfunded schools. And so, many years ago I came to the conclusion that my contribution to the field would be my efforts to change these conditions by preparing teachers who were passionate about and committed to becoming excellent teachers of marginalized students, advocates for social justice, and change agents in schools and in the lives of underachieving students—that is, I wanted to help prepare "carriers of the torch."

Lately, the teachers in my teacher education program have been telling me that, as they put it, they're not interested in going into poor schools or working with students from diverse racial, ethnic, or linguistic backgrounds—urban schools have too many problems. One preservice teacher told me, "I have no intentions of teaching *those students*. My mom works in an inner-city school and you couldn't pay me enough to work there." I was almost ready to throw in the towel when I remembered my work with Nomha.

As I began to teach my professional development course on preparing teachers for diversity at the University of Cape Town, my attention was immediately drawn to a student in the class, named Nomha. She was a very quiet, traditional, Black South African female student—reluctant to express her ideas at first, and certainly reluctant to express her ideas in aggressive or passionate ways that might threaten any of the male students in the class. It just wouldn't be culturally appropriate. Yet from the first day of class, I could see an attentiveness and intensity in Nomha's eyes that signaled that she was listening, she was thinking, she was planning, she was with me every step of the way. Over the course of the term, Nomha engaged with theory and with best practices for teaching marginalized students. As the course proceeded, I began to notice in her written work and oral discussions that she was beginning to develop a commitment to helping her students to develop "voice," as discussed by McElroy-Johnson (1993) in our teacher education course. She quoted liberally from the articles we read. And as she concentrated on helping her students to develop voice, I could see that her own voice was beginning to emerge. Although it was not my intention to change the accepted cultural practices within this South African context, by the end of the course, Nomha had developed plans of action with extended discussion about ways to allow her students to write and speak their ideas and feelings. In her final correspondence to me, Nomha thanked me for coming to South Africa to teach in the Further Diploma in Education program and for exposing her to these new ideas. In her words, "I have changed totally . . . "

Nomha helped me to remember the work I'd shared with teachers such as Gafumbe, Mieko, Mosola, Monica, Niko, Jim, Irene, and many others enrolled in my teacher education courses. Remembering these teachers helped to renew my spirit, revive my determination, and refresh my memory that teacher education programs can and are making a difference. And so I am writing this book to share the voices of such teachers and to share the details of an exploratory study—an action research project in a global context—that I conducted to demonstrate and make clear how sociocultural theory can be used as the basis for designing courses that make a difference in facilitating the development of teachers who have a commitment to teaching racially, ethnically, and linguistically diverse students in today's global society. In this book I share the story—through the voices of eight developing teachers—of a course I taught in South Africa and the United States to facilitate the development of teachers who are carriers of the torch.

In Chapter 1, I begin by discussing the challenge that currently lies before teacher education programs and propose that we need to take a global perspective on the nature of that challenge. I also share my understanding of the issues facing teacher education today and the critical role of teacher efficacy in helping educators to address the needs of marginalized students from racial, ethnic, and linguistic backgrounds that differ from their own. I implore those who would take on the challenge of teaching these students to consider the notion of *transformative academic knowledge* (Banks, 1996) and to develop voices of their own that will guide them in the generative and creative work that lies before them. In Chapter 2, I introduce readers to one perspective on the history of educational marginalization that is common both to disenfranchised minorities in the United States and to the disenfranchised majority in South Africa. In this chapter it becomes clear that the common denominator linking the experiences of Blacks in these two countries is a legacy of racial discrimination and unequal access to education. Selected historical highlights are presented to provide readers with some understanding of past events that have necessitated this exploratory study involving U.S. and South African teachers. Chapter 3 elaborates on experiences that are shared by Black populations across national boundaries. Although South African and U.S. contexts are, of course, quite different, striking similarities emerge in the themes of narratives shared by the U.S. and South African teachers and students in the study, providing insights into "what counts" as meaningful learning experiences that have shaped the educational lives of South African and U.S. learners. These narratives also reveal what these learners consider to be the important characteristics of an effective teacher.

In Chapter 4, I present a theoretical model that builds on sociocultural theory to frame the discussions that are developed throughout the rest of the book. Building on this model, I discuss the design of the research I conducted and the course on which this book is based. The model that I present has four phases, which depict the process of change experienced by the South African and U.S. teachers in my course and the changing discourse patterns that occurred as their ideologies and perspectives on teaching changed. In this chapter, I also introduce the eight focus teachers whose voices give life to the model I have presented, as they provide evidence of their changing perspectives through the written texts they have produced. The voices of these teachers unfold in the remaining four chapters of the book. These teachers' movement through each of the four phases of the model was facilitated by their use of writing as a pedagogical tool that motivated their engagement in critical inquiry and generative, reflective thought.

In Chapters 5, 6, and 7, I give detailed examples that illustrate the first three phases in the Model of Teacher Change, presented in Chapter 4. I explain in Chapter 5 how and why I used writing as a pedagogical tool to facilitate the teachers' development. The reflections and narratives of three focus teachers demonstrate how writing was used to promote teacher development. The writing samples that I share provide illustrations of the first phase of the model and shows how teachers used writing as a catalyst for generative thinking that resulted in an awakening to the important role that literacy plays in their lives and in the lives of others. In Chapter 6, I elaborate on

Phase 2 of the model and demonstrate how writing facilitates teachers' ideo-logical change. Rich examples drawn from teachers' journals provide illus-trations of how the process of ideological becoming (Bakhtin, 1981) can occur through teaching and reflection on that teaching through writing. Chapter 7 focuses on Phase 3 of the model and tells how the teachers' engagement with writing supported them through the process of internalization (Vygotsky, 1981)—a process of cognitive change—which in turn resulted in the teach-ers' development of personal voice, a sense of professional efficacy, and plans for action in their classrooms. As teachers were challenged to question their preconceived notions about diversity and as they engaged in thought-pro-voking encounters with theory, they went through a process of internaliza-tion, which facilitated the development of generative plans of action and a sense of efficacy as they contemplated becoming change agents in their schools.

In Chapter 8 I elaborate on Phase 4 of the model and share the teach-ers' insights concerning the effect of the course on their personal and profes-sional development and their day-to-day practices. Through the focus on teachers' voices, I invite readers to rethink teaching and learning for those who are preparing to teach students from diverse racial, ethnic, and language groups. The experiences they have had in schools with students of color and children of poverty give validity to the voices they share on the reform of teacher education programs that hope to prepare teachers for diversity. Their voices provide evidence that they are becoming carriers of the torch—that is, teachers who have a sense of efficacy and the attitudes, dispositions, and skills necessary to teach students from diverse racial, ethnic, and linguistic backgrounds.

Acknowledgments

A S I SHARE the voices of these teachers, I am reminded that the research, writing, and editing of this book could not have been accomplished without the generous help of many people and institutions. I would like to thank Magdalena Esterhuizen, my South African friend and colleague, for inviting me to South Africa and for teaching me about the languages and customs of the people of her country. I'd also like to thank her family, Auntie Joe, Martin, Isabelle, Henry, Amado, and Clarisa, for opening their hearts and their homes to me as I taught and learned in the universities and townships of South Africa. I will be forever grateful to the director of the Project for the Study of Alternative Education in South Africa (PRAESA), Dr. Neville Alexander, and the program's outstanding faculty and staff—Carole Bloch, Kathleen Heugh, Babazile Mahlalela, Thabile Mbatha, Naledi Mbude, Peter Plüddemann, and Zola Wababa—who allowed me the opportunity to participate in their wonderful program, which is bringing innovation to language policy, curriculum, and education in South Africa and providing groundbreaking insights on multilingual education to the global community. Also, many thanks to Lyn Taitz for allowing me to co-teach her class at what was then called Johannesburg College of Education. I greatly appreciated the opportunity to teach with these dedicated people and I thank them for their support and guidance and for allowing me to work with their students. Most important, I'd like to express my gratitude to the South African and American teachers with whom I was privileged to have the opportunity to work. Without their compassion and openness, I could never have completed this research.

A number of colleagues offered helpful advice over the course of this multiyear study. I'd like to express my thanks to Shirley Brice Heath, James Banks, Courtney Cazden, Carol Lee, Gloria Ladson-Billings, Marilyn Chambliss, Roberta Herter, Jim Wertsch, John Baugh, Geneva Smitherman, Roland Tharp, Lester Monts, Ron Marx, Sarah Freedman, Jackie Irvine, and Michelle Foster for their helpful advice, for their encouragement, and for being such wonderful colleagues. Some of them read and commented on segments of the manuscript at various stages of its development, for which I am very grateful. I often, but not always, followed the advice of these highly valued friends and colleagues. Consequently, they deserve much of the credit for the strengths of the book but bear no responsibility for its shortcomings. The following then University of Michigan graduate students—now most are professional colleagues—assisted with the data collection and its organization and synthesis: Kimberley Broussard, James Valbrun, Victoria Emika, Thandeka Chapman, Delvin Dinkins, and Janae Townsand. Thanks also to Andrea Christensen and Laurie Stapleton at Stanford University for their editorial assistance and wonderful suggestions, to Romaine Perin for meticulous copy editing, and to Lyn Grossman of Teachers College Press.

My husband, Fred, deserves many thanks and lots of credit for his patience and his untiring love, for gently accepting the disruptions in our lives that the pursuit of this book entailed, and for his wisdom and advice concerning every aspect of the development of this project. I would like to thank my daughters, Alina Sharaa Ball, Anika Sangai Ball Anthony, and Ayana N'eko Ball-Griffie, for all their support. Ayana was one of my biggest cheerleaders, and Alina offered tireless encouragement and many hours of typing. In the midst of working on her own doctorate at the University of Michigan, Anika took the time to help me edit drafts of the manuscript. My daughters' insightful and scholarly suggestions and critiques, meticulous editing, and faith in the value of the contributions of this project were invaluable to me during "the last miles home" on this project. I would like to thank my sisters and brother, Mary Williams, Geraldine Bonner, Linda Ellis, and James Mathews III, and my mom and dad for their continuing support and their prayers and encouragement throughout this journey. I'd also like to thank my grandaughters, Briana, Giavanna, and Gabriella, for the loving inspiration they have provided me. If I can make some contribution toward the improvement of education for all students, this will have an impact on their educational experiences as well. They have reinspired me with a vision and genuine belief that an excellent teaching force can and will someday exist in all schools that serve all students, including those from diverse racial, ethnic, and linguistic backgrounds.

Finally, I am grateful to the Spencer Foundation, the National Council of Teachers of English, and the University of Michigan for the funding they provided to support this research. I take full responsibility, for the findings and opinions expressed in this book.

The Global Challenge of Preparing Teachers for Diversity: A Legacy of Educational Access Denied

G LOBALIZATION, TECHNOLOGICAL ADVANCES, and the increasing number of students in classrooms worldwide who are from various racial, cultural, and linguistic backgrounds make multicultural and multilingual education an imperative in the 21st century. In particular, changing demographics in rural and urban areas around the globe pose special challenges to today's teachers and to the teacher education programs that prepare them for the classrooms they will enter. The 2000 U.S. census indicated that about one out of four Americans was a person of color; that 38% of the nation's school populations would be students of color by 2005; and that by 2050, 47% will be students of color. Globally, these figures are much higher—students of color constitute well over 50% of the world's school population. The 1996 South African census statistics indicate that about 9 out of 10 South Africans are persons of color, and more than three quarters (77%) of these South Africans are classified as African/Black. Teachers, however, continue to primarily come from backgrounds that are different from those of their students, and they feel woefully underprepared to teach students from cultural and linguistic groups that differ from their own. Reports on educational achievement in South Africa and the United States show, respectively, that large numbers of Black South Africans and persons of African descent in the United States attend schools in poor, underresourced areas and that many of these students are failing to achieve at their full potential. Clearly, an important goal of teacher education in the 21st century is to prepare teachers to teach culturally and linguistically diverse students, many of whom are poor, marginalized, and underachieving.

I was motivated to write this book because I wanted to share the voices of the South African and U.S. teachers I worked with from 1994 to 2005—teachers who were preparing to teach in today's changing schools. Their voices contain important messages concerning popular practices in the preparation of teachers. I also wanted to engage teachers, teacher educators, and policy makers in a dialogue about *how* to meet the challenge of preparing teachers to teach students from diverse racial, ethnic, and language groups—students who come from a wide range of cultural, linguistic, and socioeconomic backgrounds. In essence, this book is about educational reform. Its purpose is to share a message about my efforts to prepare teachers to become change agents—"carriers of the torch"—in today's schools.

Christine Sleeter (2001a, 2001b), in looking at the research on preparing teachers to teach historically underserved students, notes that some important needs have not yet been addressed. She argues that teacher education programs must explore ways to instill positive attitudes in their preservice teachers, since having positive attitudes concerning students is a critically important factor in becoming effective teachers of historically underserved students. However, Sleeter's (2001a) review of the research revealed that

> studies suggest that a multicultural course may have an influence on students' attitudes, although we do not know under what conditions or how long the effect will persist . . . [R]esearchers . . . have used survey research on attitude change as a tool to persuade others of the value of multicultural education coursework. However, there is a need to clarify what to expect from such coursework. . . . We need, rather, to focus on preservice teachers' classroom performance in schools in which children of color and children from poverty backgrounds are clustered and to investigate what happens in preservice programs that significantly develops their teaching. (pp. 219–220)

In the present book, I report the results of a cross-national, action research exploratory study of a teacher education course designed to instill critical thinking and positive attitudes in teachers. I document the teacher participants' perspectives on the changes in their discourse, attitudes, and behavior that occurred during and following the course, and I interpret those perspectives and changes from a theoretical perspective. I report here on a study involving South African and American teachers that responds to Sleeter's plea for research on preservice teachers' classroom performance in schools in which students of color and students from poverty backgrounds are clustered and share what happened to these teachers in a teacher education course that significantly developed their teaching. The study included phenomenological research that, as Sleeter (2001a) advocates, provides "a valuable complement to positivist research" through descriptions of learning and narratives that share the teachers' perspectives on activities that took place both during and following the course. In addition, this research contributes to our understanding of the processes of teacher change. It demonstrates how a teacher education program can foster the development of teacher discourses that reflect informed, positive attitudes about diversity among teachers using writing as a pedagogical tool to motivate, facilitate, and document teacher change.

In the chapters that follow, I share the voices of both American and South African teachers with whom I have worked over the past decade—teachers who were in the midst of becoming agents of change in the lives of students from diverse cultural and linguistic groups. The stories, told through the inscribed reflections of these teachers, illustrate their personal journeys as they used writing as a pedagogical strategy. The stories combine their reflection, introspection, critique, and active engagement with the theory I presented to them, with carefully designed teaching practices they encountered, and with reflective semiotic activities strategically presented to them in our classes. Through these teachers' texts, I share the developmental journeys they took on the road to becoming carriers of the torch.

This book brings together my 10-year program of research in the United States and South Africa and reports on my efforts as a teacher educator to develop a powerful course that facilitates the development of teachers who envision themselves in the process of becoming effective teachers of students from diverse racial, ethnic, and language groups.

THE CHALLENGE

As we enter a new millennium, students from diverse racial, ethnic, and language groups across the globe are seeking access to quality educational opportunities. These students, however, are increasingly different in background and culture from one another and from their teachers. The South African population increased from 44,800,000 in 2001 to 45,026,000 in 2003 (UNICEF, 2005). According to the UN Population Division, the South African population under 18 years of age was estimated to be 17,770,000 in 2003, with an average annual urban growth rate of 2.7%. The school-age population, which was 11,941,000 in 1998, was reported to be growing annually at a rate of 1.7 percent. By 2003, the school enrollment rates reported by the UNESCO Institute of Statistics were 90% for primary school students and 65% for secondary school students. School enrollment in the primary grades increased from 6,951,777 in 1990 to 7,971,770 in 1994, and secondary school enrollment increased from 2,743,184 to 3,571,395 over the same period. During this period, the primary school teaching staff decreased from 270,365 to 213,890 (58% female), and the secondary school teaching staff increased from 113,215 to 128,784 (63% to 64% female). On the basis of these figures, it appears that student-teacher ratios increased from 26:1 to 37:1 in primary schools and from 24:1 to 27:1 in secondary schools. In 2003, the primary student-teacher ratio was reported as 35:1 (UNESCO, 2005).

In reality, however, class size in many South African townships and rural schools often ranges from 40 to 60 students. Large class size may be one of the primary contributing factors to the increased incidence of adult illiteracy in South Africa—growing from 423,400 in 1980 to 473,100 in 1995. According to Moodley and Adam (2003), living conditions and access to education, health, water, and electricity in postapartheid South Africa have improved considerably. However, it must be noted that "education management has *slowly* improved its capacity, given the legacy of past neglect and differential allocation of resources" (p. 162). This is understandable in light of Jansen's (2001) claim that South African educational practices have not changed in large part because the policies stated often are not intended to change practice but rather to achieve a broad political symbolism to mark the shift from apartheid to postapartheid society (pp. 271–272). Even though a new national curriculum program, Curriculum 2005 (C2005 Review Committee, 2000), was launched in March 1997, introducing outcome-based education, the challenge of preparing teachers to implement this curriculum has never been adequately addressed. Thus, it is no surprise that the challenge still remains for South Africa to implement a program of teacher education designed to prepare a teaching force to address the needs of its increasingly diverse student body.

In the U.S. context, it is widely recognized that the cultural gap between children in the nation's biggest schools and the teachers who teach there is large and growing. The National Education Association (1997) reported that the percentage of White teachers in the United States grew from 88% in 1971 to 91.7% in 1996, whereas the number of Black teachers decreased from 8.4% to 6.3%, and those classified as "others" have decreased from 3.6% to 2.0% during the same period. The U.S. Department of Education reported that the enrollment in public elementary and secondary schools was 63% White and 37% students of color—including 17% Black, 15% Hispanic, 4% Asian/Pacific Islander, and 1% American Indian/Alaskan Native (National Center for Education Statistics, 1999–2000). In contrast, the teaching force was reported as 84% White and 16% teachers of color—including 9% Black, 5% Hispanic, 1% Asian/Pacific Islander, and 1% American Indian/Alaskan Native. These figures indicate that large numbers of White teachers will need to be prepared with the attitudes, skills, knowledge, and dispositions necessary for teaching students from racial, ethnic, and linguistic backgrounds that differ from their own.

These global trends confirm that the demographics of our student populations are becoming more diverse, while the composition of the teaching force is becoming more monocultural. At one time, teaching Black South African children was one of the few professional careers open to highly qualified Black South Africans. In recent years, however, a broad range of occupations have opened to these highly qualified individuals, and many who at one time would have entered the teaching profession are now entering careers in business, politics, medicine, and other areas. Among those individuals who do complete a teacher education program, few are provided with the skills necessary for effectively teaching students from diverse racial, ethnic, and language groups. In many schools around the globe, teachers are asked to teach students who have life experiences that are very different from their own, and they feel unprepared to do so. However, in an extensive review of changes in teacher education programs over 2 decades, Gollnick (1995) found few substantive changes related to preparing teachers for diversity. Thus, the problem of educating teachers to teach students who come from backgrounds that differ from their own promises to pose a continuing challenge for teacher education programs into the foreseeable future.

THE GLOBAL NATURE OF THE CHALLENGE

Many educators, administrators, policy makers, and students worldwide lament the fact that schools are having relatively little success in educating students who are poor; members of socially, culturally, or racially marginalized and disenfranchised groups; and speakers of first languages that differ from the mainstream or academic varieties of English. Test score data in South Africa and the United States confirm this reality. In both countries, Black students in particular are failing to meet optimum levels of achievement. In South Africa, the majority of students who fit this description live in rural and township areas. In the United States a large majority of poor, marginalized, and underachieving African American students live in inner-city and urban areas and in the Southern regions of the United States. All could benefit from well-trained, culturally competent teachers who could apply their cultural knowledge to the teaching of diverse students.

In South Africa, Blacks make up the majority population in the society and in the schools. They constitute more than 75% of the population. Just over 50% of South Africans now live in urban areas, while the rural population is decreasing because of rural–urban migration. Banks (1991) observed more than a decade ago that in the United States, those who had traditionally been considered minorities were becoming the majority population in many of our nation's largest cities. At that time, 50 of the largest 99 school districts in the country had enrollments of more than 50% students of color (National Center for Educational Statistics, 1994). By 2001, 40% of the students enrolled in public schools were students of color.

Today, more than half of public school students in the nation's larger cities (Washington, DC; Los Angeles; Chicago; New York; and San Francisco) are students of color, and five majority-minority states exist. This increase primarily results from growth in the Latino student population. In 1998–1999, students of color made up 63.1% of the public school population in California, the nation's largest state (California State Department of Education, 2000). The majority of African American and Latino students living within the nation's largest metropolitan areas attend schools that are characterized as underresourced, urban, or central-city public schools. When comparing such schools with more affluent suburban schools, Orfield and Reardon (1993) discovered profound differences in the quality of educational opportunity and the teaching staff, with underresourced schools functioning at a grossly inferior level. This is the case for schools in South Africa as well.

It is not surprising to find that students in disadvantaged schools score lower on standardized achievement tests and matriculation exams than do their more affluent counterparts and that they drop out at higher rates than those in advantaged schools. After analyzing the nature and extent of these inequities, Orfield and Reardon (1993) concluded:

> If these schools lack certified teachers, offer few academically challenging courses, and track disadvantaged students disproportionately into low-level courses; if the community is economically depressed, with few libraries, museums, and other non-school educational opportunities; and if a large number of adults with high school diplomas are unable to find adequate employment; then we cannot in good conscience claim that many disadvantaged students have simply failed to do what it takes to succeed in school. Rather, our society has failed to give them the opportunity to succeed. These students have not failed school; society has failed them. (p. 29)

Despite the considerable rhetoric about school restructuring, the majority of non-White students in South Africa and the United States, and particularly Black students, are faring very poorly academically when compared with Whites, and the former are more likely to be attending underresourced schools. Thus, the challenge remains for us to prepare teachers who can teach underrepresented, marginalized students effectively and who have a desire to do so. According to Orfield and Reardon (1993),

> Young teachers working in high poverty . . . schools find the job less rewarding and are more likely to consider leaving teaching. As a result, schools serving poor and minority children often hire less-qualified teachers than advantaged schools. . . . Minority and low-income students tend to be in schools and school districts with . . . less well prepared teachers and counselors [who have] larger class sizes. (p. 24)

As these inequitable situations become more widely known and less tolerated, educational reformers are challenging teacher-preparation programs to adequately equip student teachers to have the knowledge, attitudes, and skills to work effectively with students who are culturally and linguistically diverse (Carnegie Council on Adolescent Development, 1989; Darling-Hammond, 1986; Hartshorne, 1992; Irvine, 2003; Quality Education for Minority Project, 1990; Rosenholtz, 1986).

In order to address this challenge two things must occur. First, it is necessary to investigate both approaches that motivate teachers to consider the option of teaching students from diverse racial, ethnic, and language groups in marginalized schools and the mechanisms through which teachers become more confident about their sense of teacher efficacy—that is, about their ability to teach all students effectively. Second, it is important that teachers be exposed to transformative academic knowledge in their teacher education programs. According to Banks (1996), "Transformative academic knowledge consists of concepts, paradigms, themes, and explanations that challenge mainstream knowledge" and further challenges mainstream notions of the purpose of knowledge (p. 16). Teachers who are influenced by transformative academic knowledge realize that knowledge is not neutral, that it reflects power and social relationships within society, and that an important purpose of knowledge construction is to help people improve society (Code, 1991; Harding, 1991; hooks & West, 1991). King and Mitchell (1990) note, "Like other praxis oriented critical approaches, the Afrocentric method [one example of transformative academic knowledge] seeks to enable people to understand social reality in order to change it. But its additional imperative is to transform the society's basic ethos" (p. 95). Transformative academic knowledge plays a critical role in our efforts to prepare teachers to work with students who are culturally and linguistically diverse and who attend under-resourced schools. Such knowledge serves to prepare them not only to teach these students effectively, but also to influence change in the socioeconomically based inequalities reflected in the conditions of the schools they work in. The perspectives that these teachers take on through transformative academic knowledge gives purpose and direction to the efficacy that teachers are developing.

TEACHER EFFICACY

In my work with teachers I have come to recognize that efficacy plays a key role in the development of teachers who work effectively with students from diverse racial, ethnic, and linguistic backgrounds. The concept of teacher efficacy in the education literature has generally emerged from Bandura's "self-efficacy" theories (Bandura, 1977, 1986, 1997). The term *teacher efficacy* refers to a teacher's belief in his or her potential ability to affect positive change in the lives of his or her students and to a teacher's expectation that he or she can help students learn in any given situation (Ashton & Webb, 1986; Pang & Sablan, 1995). It has been argued that a teacher's sense of efficacy is critical to his or her effectiveness in the classroom. The Rand study conducted by Berman, McLaughlin, Bass, Pauly, and Zellman (1977) was the first research to include a construct for teachers' sense of efficacy as a variable in measuring the success of educational reforms and innovations. The research team found surprisingly high correlations between a teachers' sense of efficacy and student achievement, success of innovation, adoption of new curricula, and durability of innovation (also see Ashton & Webb, 1986; Rosenholtz, 1989). Since the Rand study, researchers have sought to refine the concept and better measure efficacy in an attempt to understand the types of interventions that would enhance teacher efficacy and thus presumably raise educational quality (Ashton & Webb, 1986; Gibson & Dembo, 1984; Guskey, 1988; Malarkey, 1992; Tschannen-Moran, Woolfolk Hoy, & Hoy, 1998, 2001).

Teacher efficacy plays a particularly critical role when we consider the development of teachers who would work with students at risk of educational failure; low-achieving students are particularly sensitive to their teachers' sense of efficacy (Midgely, Feldlaufer, & Eccles, 1989). The Rand study found that the scores of minority students were more strongly affected by teacher efficacy than were those of their white peers (Berman et al., 1977). Likewise, teachers who have a low sense of efficacy when working with lower-achieving students generally have a much more difficult time producing the results they want and thus develop a lower sense of efficacy concerning the situation (Hannaway, 1990). Hannaway points out that with "at-risk" students, a multiplier effect can occur between poor student achievement and low teacher efficacy—the two affect each other negatively in a downward spiral of educational quality.

Low teacher efficacy among the teachers of Black students is of particular concern. It has been correlated with teachers' low expectations when working with these students (Gibson & Dembo, 1984) and with less persistence by teachers who work with students who are struggling (Ashton & Webb, 1986). In essence, it seems that the lower a teacher's sense of efficacy, the more he or she will avoid situations where success is perceived to be doubtful (Ashton & Webb, 1986). This is often the case among teachers who work in schools that serve poor, marginalized, and underachieving students, and particularly in schools that serve predominantly Black populations.

From the work of Grant and Secada (1990) and Gomez (1993), we know that the predominant teaching force consists of young, White, middle-class females who are often assigned to schools and classrooms that serve students from diverse racial, ethnic, and language groups—sites where their more experienced colleagues do not wish to teach. Often these teachers find themselves working with students they had no intention of teaching, and teaching in situations where they are least prepared by their university programs to teach. These teachers often bring to the classroom perspectives, attitudes, and beliefs that can be a major barrier to the effective teaching of diverse students. For many novice teachers, one major barrier to effective instruction is the belief that many students of color are not capable of learning as effectively as are their White peers. This has a negative effect on both teacher efficacy and student achievement. Teachers with high personal teaching efficacy—those who feel they have the power to produce an effect on their students—believe that all students can be motivated and that it is their responsibility to explore with students the tasks that hold their attention and facilitate learning. When we apply this information to the need to prepare teachers to teach diverse students, a question arises: How can teachers come to understand and internalize this powerful view of teacher efficacy? This book is, in part, a response to that question.

In my own career I have encountered many teacher educators who recognize the importance of teacher efficacy, but this is expressed as a hope that their students will simply possess efficacy or develop it somewhere along the way. These teacher educators often feel that they are not doing enough to help dispel teachers' feelings of inadequacy, pessimism, frustration, helplessness, and resistance around issues of diversity. Often, teacher educators recognize policy and programmatic limitations to instilling a sense of efficacy in their teachers, or to preparing them to become the change agents needed in our public schools. Those of us who focus specifically on teaching courses that are designed to address the need for an adequate supply and equal distribution of qualified teachers to serve diverse student populations (Darling-Hammond, 1996) sometimes experience an uneasy feeling that we, too, are not influencing teachers in the ways we would like. We know that if we are to become more effective at preparing teachers as agents of change, we must examine more closely the processes and mechanisms of teacher change and effective ways to facilitate the development of a teaching force that will accelerate needed reforms. This book addresses these issues.

THE RESEARCH JOURNEY

In 1994, I received a call from a close friend and colleague who invited me to travel to South Africa to investigate issues of educational change and reform. I had completed several years of teaching in a teacher education program in an American university. My research had examined language practices and literacy learning in a wide range of formal and informal learning environments, focusing primarily on how teachers could better understand the linguistic practices of marginalized students and draw on those language practices as a resource in their teaching (Ball, 1992, 1995a, 1995b, 1998b, 2000, 2002; Ball & Farr, 2003; Ball & Lardner, 1997, 2005). My work had also focused on community-based organizations as alternative contexts where poor and marginalized populations were experiencing successful learning (Ball, 1995b). I looked at these environments as models for educational reform and planned to expand that line of study in schools and nongovernmental organizations (NGOs) in South Africa.

During my first visit to South Africa, in 1994, I conducted a broad investigation of literacy practices in schools and community-based organizations and the role of language in community building—which paralleled my prior work in the United States. I conducted interviews and observations in more than 40 educational institutions—from NGOs and underresourced rural and township schools to the elite, formerly White schools. And just as in the United States, I encountered teachers who had a passion and love for teaching students from diverse backgrounds, and teachers who developed rich, productive learning environments for students from diverse racial, ethnic, and language groups—often despite the underresourced working conditions. Unfortunately, I also had many encounters with teachers who lacked the ability to interact effectively with culturally and linguistically diverse students and who were frustrated by the failure and miscommunication that marked their experiences with socially and economically disenfranchised students.

During one of my visits to a formerly White school (which at that time served mostly upper-class, English-speaking students), I observed similarities in the educational experiences of students of color in the United States and in South Africa: I was approached by an Afrikaans-speaking student who asked, "Do you think that I am dumb?" Thinking that I must have heard him incorrectly, I asked him to repeat himself. He responded, "You know . . . do you think I'm stupid because of my Afrikaans accent . . . because of the way I talk?" Like many students in the United States, this student felt that his intelligence was being judged by the way he spoke. He was obviously the victim of what John Baugh refers to as *linguistic profiling*. I realized then that many South African students were facing intense social, political, and educational dilemmas that were similar to those of dialect speakers and English-language learners in the United States. These issues of social, educational, and political consequence are not unique to the United States—indeed, they are universal, and the lessons we can learn from studying them can be beneficial in cross-national contexts.

During my second extended visit to South Africa, in 1995, I was invited to serve as an academic specialist and to consult with members of NGOs and agencies on researching aspects of teacher education and curriculum development. While teaching courses to preservice and in-service teachers from multicultural and multilingual settings, I was struck by the similarities in the challenges I faced as an instructor in my South African and American teacher education classrooms. In both contexts, education was going through massive reform and restructuring programs. Having similar histories of segregated schooling for marginalized populations, both countries were now suffering the consequences of earlier decisions to subject large groups of people to educational inequity. However, while the fruits of reform in the teaching profession were apparent in the increasingly impressive qualifications and abilities of teachers in advantaged communities, a countervailing trend in both countries was a growing population of underprepared teachers working in underserved communities. Armed with little knowledge about teaching and how their students learned, they were entering classrooms to teach their nation's poor and diverse student populations. Also in both countries, this problem was rooted in the failure of government, policy makers, and teacher education programs to address the need for an adequate supply and equal distribution of qualified teachers to serve all students in all areas.

During my 1995 visit to South Africa, I became interested in expanding my explorations into questions about the process of teacher development, about how teachers move toward becoming change agents, and about how writing can be used as a pedagogical tool for inquiry and critique in preparing teachers to teach racially, ethnically, and linguistically diverse students. South Africa provided a new and exciting context and many parallels with the United States. In both countries I encountered teachers who were interested in teaching students much like themselves, and who ultimately decided not to engage in teaching students who were poor, underachieving, and attending under-resourced schools. Motivated by a determination to better understand these processes, I developed a project to investigate whether teachers' discourses, practices, and views about teaching diverse students could be positively influenced by engagement with a carefully planned course designed to facilitate teacher commitment and efficacy. Through careful study and contemplation, I determined that this would need to involve teachers in directed experiences with action research as they engaged in teaching activities with diverse students; extensive use of writing as a pedagogical tool for inquiry and critique; strategic exposure to sociocultural theory that supports sound practice; and engaging discussions that challenged preconceived notions about diversity.

In 1995 and 1997, I applied these principles in the courses I taught in the United States, at a teacher education program in Guatang province, and in a Further Diploma in Education program in Cape Town. My decision to focus on teacher education in my research, and specifically on the process of teacher change, grew out of my recurring experiences with students in my own American university teacher education program and now in these South

African teacher education programs, as well. In both contexts I found student teachers who initially came into my classroom interested in attaining a credential to teach students who were much like themselves. For many reasons, a high percentage of these teachers ultimately decided not to engage in teaching students from diverse racial, ethnic, and language groups. A high percentage of these teachers were uninterested in teaching students who were poor, underachieving, or attending underresourced schools. Some of the teachers were unconvinced of the power and potential of teacher education programs to adequately prepare them to teach these students. Others were simply uninterested in dealing with issues of becoming teachers of students from diverse backgrounds. Their line of reasoning seemed to be, Why would I come to a top-ranked research institution to become prepared to work with students who are poor, marginalized, and underachieving? I came here with visions of teaching students who are much like me—the best and the brightest. My initial reactions to such logic were alarm and frustration, which evolved into a research focus when I learned of other studies reporting that this outlook was not unusual on the part of preservice and some in-service teachers. As I considered these issues, it became clear to me that since we live in a global society, we have global educational challenges, which could most effectively be addressed through studies of teacher change and development that were not limited by national boundaries.

I further recognized that no longer could the challenge to prepare teachers to teach all students—to prepare an adequate supply and equitable distribution of qualified teachers—be narrowly conceptualized as a local problem, or as an urban or rural one. The challenge was truly global, requiring a wide understanding of the processes of teacher change. It would therefore require cross-national studies that investigated how teachers moved from being simply teachers committed to teaching, to become educators empowered with a vision of what it means to be committed to teaching *all* students. It would require research that contributed to the development of teachers empowered through a strong sense of efficacy—a quality that is required of all educators who hope to become successful teachers of culturally and linguistically diverse populations. Such were the foci of the teacher education courses I taught in South Africa and the United States.

THE JOURNEY BEGINS

At the turn of the millenium, I had taught in teacher education programs in the United States since 1992. During seven extended visits to South Africa (1994–2005), I provided workshops and lectures to parents, teachers, university students, and scholars interested in the education of youths who were at risk of educational failure. I also collected data on language, literacy, and learning in formal and informal schools and in community-based organizations and conducted a cross-national study of teacher development and change. I gave lectures at Witwatersrand University, the University of South Africa (UNISA), the University of Natal, and the University of Zululand and taught extended courses at the University of Cape Town and what was then called Johannesburg College of Education.

In the year 2000, just 9 days after the dawning of the New Year, I kissed my husband and three daughters good-bye and boarded a plane at San Francisco International Airport for Amsterdam, where I connected with a transcontinental flight bound for South Africa. My project was to expand on my U.S. research into how teachers change and develop over time. As I sat on the airplane, I recalled my experience on the first day of class in the Further Diploma in Education course I had taught in South Africa 3 years earlier. As I surveyed the 1997 classroom during our introductory class, I looked into the warm, friendly student faces. I noticed, however, that one face stood out in the crowd. It was that of a skeptic—with piercing eyes, clenched jaw, and arms crossed firmly across his chest. I later learned that this student's name was Gafumbe. After introducing myself to the class and describing the type of research I was interested in conducting, I asked, "Do any of you have questions that you would like to ask me?" Gafumbe raised his hand and spoke: "Why should we openly share our ideas and thoughts with you? For what purpose? And what are you planning to do with the research that you collect? Many foreigners have come to South Africa to study us, and then they leave and we hear nothing from them after that. Why should we expect you to be any different?"

Gafumbe's question opened the door for me to share my observation that people of color, and particularly Blacks, were experiencing very similar challenges, in the United States, South Africa, and other cross-national contexts in our struggle to attain quality education and upward mobility within a global society. Over time, through a change in attitude, disposition, and ideological stance, Gafumbe began to have changed perceptions about my work. This is how he described his thoughts at the end of the course:

> As time went by, I realized that you were not just another educationist, but you were a concerned learner. The problems that we are faced with—it dawned in my mind—are problems that African Americans, South Africans, and basically people of the whole world are faced with in regard to the learning and acquisition of additional languages. Your overt and covert objectives have been clarified for me as we have progressed through this class . . . I have—during the course of your stay—come to realize the importance of literacy to all people . . .

As the course progressed, it became clear to Gafumbe and to the rest of the class that my purpose in coming to South Africa was to learn from them about how teachers could develop a sense of efficacy and become change agents in their schools. My desire was to act as a vehicle for sharing that information with the larger educational community through the teachers' own voices. This book is a realization of that goal.

IN CONCLUSION

While international concern about preparing teachers for a diverse student population is increasing, research confirms that the teacher education profession as a whole has been moving *very slowly* toward an internalization of the principles of multicultural education. It should be noted that even the term *multicultural education* is a contested one. In South Africa, multicultural education, named as such, was a project of the apartheid state, in which the idea of fixed identities, defined by the accident of skin color, was used to divide and exploit groups and individuals according to a state-determined hierarchy—taking the notion of "the social construction of identity" to new levels (see Carrim & Soudien, 1999; Soudien, 1998, 2004). In the United States this term is contested in a context in which nonracialism (in all its complexity) is a foundation for a new democracy. Within these contested terrains, significant progress will not be made in improving teachers' "less-than-positive responses . . . to the multicultural education [course] requirement" (King & Ladson-Billings, 1990) until the processes of teacher change and the possibilities of instilling a strong sense of efficacy in our teachers are better understood. These improved understandings should be situated within the context of a transformative knowledge-based curriculum that helps teachers and students to understand the role they can play in improving society and transforming the economic inequalities reflected in the underresourced schools in which they work and learn.

Borders and Boundaries: Common Bonds and Dissimilar Circumstances

Why This Book Focuses on South Africa and the United States

I N THIS CHAPTER, I outline some similarities and differences between the histories of teacher education in South Africa and in the United States, present congruencies between teacher and student educational experiences in both countries, and discuss teacher efficacy as an important factor influencing student learning and academic outcomes. In reviewing some historical highlights that link South African and U.S. learners across national boundaries, I make no claims of being complete or comprehensive in my account of marginalized peoples in these two vast countries. My goals, rather, are to give the reader a feel for similar challenges facing students and teachers in the two contexts and to provide background information to situate the discussions that follow. It should also be noted that these issues are relevant to other countries where classrooms are becoming increasingly diverse and where similar histories of racism, colonialism, and marginalization exist. For example, a number of countries in South America are also experiencing much greater diversity among their school populations. The important point to keep in mind is that the magnitude of the problem this book addresses is indeed global and critically important to the future of education for all students.

UNDERSTANDING THE SOCIAL AND HISTORICAL CONTEXT: A LEGACY OF SEGREGATION AND APARTHEID

In this chapter, I introduce readers to a history of educational disenfranchisement that has some remarkable similarities for the Black minority population in the United States and the majority indigenous population of Blacks in South Africa. The common denominator across the two contexts is one of racial discrimination and unequal access to education for Blacks in both countries, and the perspectives that I describe situate these two countries educationally.

Most studies of education rarely go beyond national borders. While some exceptions do exist (D. Foster & Russell, 2002; Freedman, 1994), rarely do these cross-national studies report on rich data sources situated within teacher-preparation programs that include literacy autobiographies, journal entries, classroom discussions, and videotaped classroom observations; and even rarer still is the case in which cross-national data sources focus on South African and U.S. teachers and classrooms. This book defies those trends by presenting rich data focusing on South African and U.S. educational contexts, as both countries strive to educate large numbers of poor, disenfranchised, marginalized, and underachieving students who are culturally and linguistically different from members of the dominant culture, from their teachers, and from the students generally viewed as the primary audience for whom most instructional materials and methods are tailored.

Historically, South Africa and the United States have experienced similarities in regard to relegating large populations of persons of color to segregated schooling, and they have used that schooling to subjugate African Americans and Black South Africans in particular. Practices of unequal school funding and policies that maintain inequality have plagued the schooling realities of Black students in these countries for some time. However, current reform movements and changing political, social, and economic situations in the United States and South Africa make this a historically significant time to investigate some of the common educational challenges. With an official end to apartheid and economic sanctions, barriers that once existed are now changing. South Africa has rejoined the rest of the world and reconstruction of the educational system has been under way for more than a decade. This is an opportune time to observe and document changes from which we can learn a great deal.

Dissimilar Circumstances

Possible difficulties in a cross-national study of teacher development and change in the United States and South Africa can arise from marked differences in languages, language policies, racial group dynamics, economic realities, and political systems, particularly if one assumes that the countries under study have the same systems of education—they do not. Despite their differences, we can learn many important things from a study of South Africa and the United States in regard to preparing teachers to work with racially, ethnically, and linguistically diverse students. A separate and complex comparative literature on issues of race, identity, social movements, and education in the two countries already exists (see Fredrickson, 1995, 1997, 2004; Nkomo, 1984, 1990; Omond, 1986), so I will not attempt to replicate its content. However, in reading that literature, it becomes clear that the U.S.

educational system evolved to address the educational needs of its citizens in ways that differed significantly from the South African model.

First, while religious missionary organizations played a significant role in the early educational history of Blacks in both countries, the missions' evolving participation played itself out in different ways in the two contexts. When the ascension to power of the National Party in South Africa in 1948 marked the birth of formalized apartheid, the government became intent on eliminating the controlling influence of the English-speaking mission institutions on Bantu (Black) education. Missionary colleges, which had provided an educational alternative for Blacks, were closed down or taken over by the government, and by the late 1960s teacher training as it had existed under the mission churches before apartheid had been "ruthlessly and systematically destroyed"(Hartshorne, 1992, p. 236). In the United States, following the Civil War, the foundation of the Freedmen's Bureau educational movement was the deep-seated desire of Blacks to control and sustain schools for themselves and their children. While ex-slaves accepted support from northern missionary societies, they wanted *assistance without control.* This desire for self-reliance came as a surprise to many White missionaries, and by the mid-1870s, the northern missionary associations were already reducing their involvement in Black southern education and concentrating their efforts and financial assistance primarily on normal schools and higher education. Therefore, while ex-slaves had split with their closest allies, Yankee missionaries, concerning the question of who should control educational institutions for Black children, missionary colleges were instrumental in training a large percentage of Black teachers well into the 20th century in the United States (Anderson, 1988).

While this struggle for control and ideological hegemony in the education of Blacks in the South (where the majority of Blacks were living) was occurring at the local level, the federal government did not play an overt, direct, or formal role in denying quality education to Blacks. Although it is true that the 1896 decision by the U.S. Supreme Court in the case of *Plessy v. Ferguson* legalized racial inequality and segregation for the following half century, the case did not initially focus on education. History shows, however, that its interpretation influenced more than just separate railroad cars. It led to the legitimacy of segregation for schools, restaurants, courthouses, bathrooms, and even drinking fountains for decades. This second example of a distinct difference that existed between the U.S. and South African educational contexts revolved around the roles played by officials at the national level. While local admissions policies in South Africa and the United States served to exclude most Blacks, and the curriculum established in both countries reflected a White worldview that omitted African and African American perspectives on history and literature, Blacks in South Africa were also confronted with national de facto policies that further prohibited their access to education. For example, in 1959, Parliament passed the Extension of University Education Act, which prohibited established universities from accepting Black students except through special permission of a cabinet minister.

A third important difference between these countries is that South Africa recognizes 11 official national languages in its constitution, sending a message that multilingualism is valued. The United States appears to be moving toward supporting an "English only" national policy—sending a message of *devaluing* multilingualism. As South African and U.S. classrooms become more linguistically diverse, educators are challenged daily to find ways to use students' home languages and literacies in strategic and thoughtful ways to implement more effective instructional programs. This situation is further complicated in both countries because of the numerous mismatches between the economic, social, cultural, and linguistic backgrounds of students and their teachers.

A final distinct difference in the U.S. and South African educational contexts that I will mention revolves around issues of demographics. Although similar long-standing problems in education have persisted for disenfranchised populations in both countries, Black students in South Africa are the numerical majority, as compared to the minority Black population in the United States. This has had implications for how Blacks see themselves—socially, politically, and economically—in the two countries, and in the amount of time it will take for inequities to be addressed.

Common Bonds and Similar Circumstances

Having acknowledged some of the distinct differences that exist between the South African and U.S. educational contexts, I would also stress their common bonds and similar circumstances. As Meyer and Rowen (1978) have pointed out, the structures and prevailing instructional patterns in schools around the world tend to be more similar to each other than they are different. With this in mind, I contend that it would be enlightening to highlight some of the historical similarities that emerge from a close look at South African and U.S. practices as they relate to the education of Black populations.

South Africa and the United States share some striking similarities in their histories of the education of marginalized people of color, and this is not by accident. Between World War I and World War II, the Black educational school system in the American South was considered a suitable model for the development of an educational system for Blacks in South Africa. Charles T. Loram, a South African born in 1879 and graduate of Teachers'

College, Columbia University, was a key figure among those who orches-
trated the use of U.S. educational theories and practices to provide guidance
for developing schools for Blacks in South Africa—schools that would in-
culcate African subservience to an acceptance of White authority. According to Davis (1984):

> Maurice S. Evans, then Natal's leading so-called "expert on the Native prob-
> lem," also influenced Loram to look to the United States for answers to prob-
> lems of African education. . . . Loram went to Teachers' College . . . [where]
> he was interested in studying Black schooling to learn which of its aspects were
> applicable to South Africa. . . . [He] visited Tuskegee, in addition to Hampton
> Institute, Virginia Union University, and a number of small Black schools in
> Alabama, Maryland, and Virginia, in connection with his doctoral research.
> . . . Shortly after his return to his position with the Natal education depart-
> ment, Loram won promotion to the newly created post of chief inspector of
> native education. (pp. 110–111, 113)

The work of Loram, Evans, and others explains some of the similarities that
existed between educational goals and objectives for Blacks in the United
States and Blacks in South Africa. In particular, they help to explain similarities in the articulation of the common goal geared toward entrenching
White control and superiority and Black subservience and their perception
of themselves as rural, unskilled laborers.

Institutionalizing White Superiority and White Privilege

The institutionalization of ideologies that legitimize White superiority and
justify racial segregation occurred in both the United States and South Africa.
This was accomplished through curricula that emphasized European literature and White history, excluded Black history, and distorted historical realities in subtle but pervasive ways (Jansen, 1990). In addition, both countries
have shared many of the same ideologies concerning language policies and
the mechanisms used to carry them out. The primary policy that South Africa and the United States have implemented in past years through apartheid and segregation has been a separate and unequal system of education
that deliberately miseducated the countries' Blacks in an attempt to lower
their aspirations and to prepare them for an underclass role in society. This
policy was implemented through a curriculum that failed to challenge the
higher-order thinking of Black students and emphasized practical skills-ori-
ented teaching. Prominent themes expressed throughout the literature document a history of inequity concerning the quality of schools, educational
access, and disparities in the preparation of teachers that teach Black students in both countries. These practices included the undereducation or lack

of education for Black students and gross inequities in all areas of student spending. These inequalities continue to exist in the form of racially unequal funding of schools, overcrowded classrooms, dilapidated buildings, inadequate facilities, unengaging instructional policies and practices, and underqualified teachers. The limited access to high-quality education for most Blacks results in high failure and high drop-out rates, which in turn exclude the majority of Blacks from access to postsecondary educational opportunities.

Historically, the institutionalization of societal racism was evident in schools through discriminatory hiring and promotion practices. These practices effectively excluded Blacks from meaningful economic participation. Goodenow and White (1981) argue that the goal of Southern industrialists, Northern philanthropists, and educational reformers in general was to force Blacks into a workable scheme of social organization that would permit the structuring of a caste economy. Following the abolition of slavery in the United States, the goal of the school was to help fit Blacks into that caste scheme. In the crafting of apartheid in South Africa, a similar plan was implemented. In the industrial United States, manual training was used to "keep Blacks in their place, not to offer them advancement" (Goodenow & White, 1981, pp. 125–126). In 1880s South Africa, the aim of schools was to make servants out of Blacks. Bantu education was later instituted to ensure that Black people were functionally illiterate and economically shackled. The schools taught the "master's language" and a limited vocabulary. In both countries, the educational system provided Blacks with elementary-level literacy skills and trained them in discipline and the skills of manual labor in order to build within them a feeling of inferiority—for example, a curriculum of carpentry for boys; dressmaking, cooking, and laundering for girls; and gardening for both.

In 1954, South African prime minister Hendrik Verwoerd, the ideological architect of apartheid, labeled one of his cornerstones a completely separate and different education system for Blacks. Bantu education was that cornerstone.

The African National Congress (ANC) noted that apartheid and Bantu education had left thousands of young Blacks lacking the decent education, skills, and work habits to participate constructively in the South African economy following apartheid. In the 1980s, one out of every four children dropped out of school within the first 2 years, and one out of every five Black children had no access to school. By 1989, the Black pass rate on countrywide matriculation exams (the equivalent of a high school diploma in the United States) was only 40%; it was 36% in 1990. John Samuel (1992), the ANC's director of education, noted the deliberate undereducation of Black South African children in the areas of math, science, and language. He noted that as late as 1990, of the 200,000 total student population in high school, only 12 black children obtained an A-grade pass in mathematics (Novicki 1985, p. 21).

In the early United States, the English colonies had a policy of segregation. Knowles and Prewitt (1969) have said:

> The English colonist operated from a premise, which has continued to have a strong influence on American thought. The Anglo-Saxon is culturally and religiously superior. . . . This belief was strengthened by such racist theories as the Teutonic Theory of Anglo-Saxons. The White man generally characterized Non-Whites as "disadvantaged," "unfortunate," or "culturally deprived." (p. 43)

Albert Cleage (1968), a leading member of the Black clergy, has written:

> In American society, the White schools perpetuate, and hand down from generation to generation, the White man's interpretation of the world, of history, of religion, of God, of everything. Schools are an instrument for handing down to Black children the White man's conception of the world. But you must know that the schools are vicious. They are a destructive influence on our children because they are teaching them White supremacy for the most part through the curriculum; the classes, the teachers, the books, the very power symbols, like the preponderance of White teachers and administrators. (p. 77)

Unequal Facilities and Resources

At the dawn of the 20th century in the United States, proponents of universal elementary education for Blacks recognized that nearly two thirds of Black elementary school–age children did not attend school, because there were not enough buildings or seating capacity to accommodate them and there was a shortage of teachers to teach them. There was a southern Black ratio of 93 school-age children for every teacher. Although the magnitude of this teacher shortage declined over the years, the basic pattern "remained through the first third of the twentieth century" (Anderson, 1988, p. 111; see also Watkins, 2001). By the 1940s, Black schools continued to be ill equipped, their terms shorter, their teachers poorly trained, and their instructional curricula inferior when compared to their White counterparts. In 1990, the educational situation for Blacks in poor and inner-city communities had not changed to a large degree, and college entrance rates for Blacks remained low.

In the United States, there has historically been a deprivation of adequate facilities and well-trained teachers to serve the educational needs of Black students. For the first half of the 20th century, the bulk of African American schoolchildren attended impoverished, small, short-term schools with pronounced inadequacies in every aspect of the educational program (Anderson, 1988; Walker & Archung, 2003). Even today, in practice, students attending predominantly Black schools rarely receive educational appropriations, facilities, or curricular emphasis equal to those of most White schools. In predominantly Black schools, emphasis is placed on low-level, skills-based education and on discipline, rather than on the more classical college preparatory curriculum received by a large number of Whites. Expectations for Black and White students continue to be very different. The disparity between money spent on the education of White children versus Black children is disheartening. In 1900, $3 was spent on every White child in the United States as opposed to $2 for every Black child. In 1930, $7 was spent for Whites and still only $2 for Blacks. In 1935–1936, the expenditures for White students averaged $37.87 per child, while those for Black students were $13.09 per child (Franklin & Moss, 2000, p. 406). Today, disparities continue. A recent PBS documentary revealed that many inner-city schools in California suffer serious shortcomings such as overcrowding, inadequate libraries with no librarian on site, inadequate sanitation facilities, nonfunctioning water facilities for student use, and inadequate provision of textbooks (*First to Worst*, 2003).

In South Africa, significant disparities in government spending for Black versus White students have existed in the areas of textbook allocations, school facilities, and quantity and quality of teachers (Mncwabe, 1989, 1990, 1993). In the 1930s, the government was spending over 40 times more on White pupils than on the comparable Black African population (Kallaway, 1984). During the early 1970s, government spending was 18 times more on a White student than on a Black student. In 1979, the government spent 10 times more on White students as on Black students. By 1987–88, the government spent 4.6 times more on White students than on Black students.

Clearly, the stories of Black people and their educational experiences in South Africa and the United States are deeply etched by inequality, adversity, and struggle. Notable in these stories is the perseverance of Black people in striving to attain quality education to ensure the livelihood and prosperity of future generations.

COMMON BONDS CONCERNING TEACHER PREPARATION

A closer look at the history of Black teacher education in South Africa and the United States reveals a similar second-class system of teacher education designed to keep Blacks in positions of social, political, and economic subordination.

South African Models of Teacher Education

The formal, institutional training of teachers in South Africa began in 1841 at Lovedale, an institution of the Glasgow Missionary Society that was established to train Black teachers and evangelists. In formulating teacher training programs, these early mission schools focused on instilling in Black teachers an ethic of hard work, obedience, and duty. In 1859, teacher education candidates had to be at least 13 years old; attached to a school for at least 3 years; and receive at least 4 hours of special duties a week in addition to their classroom duties, at the end of which they were allowed to enter the Third Class Teacher's Certificate program. By 1901, student teachers in the Cape went on to do a 3-year teachers' course after completing Standard 6. It was also possible to gain a Second Class Teacher's Certificate by completing a 4th and 5th year of training, which also implied that the candidate had passed the matriculation examination (high school exit exam). Only about a quarter of the students entering the 1st year completed this course. Almost all those who failed, however, went into the Black schools to teach as uncertified teachers. In 1917, Dr. C. T. Loram upgraded the standards of English in the teacher-training schools, increasing the time given to supervised practice teaching in real schools, pioneering in-service training of teachers, and instituting the Native Teachers Library and *Native Teachers Journal* as resources for Black teachers. By 1953, the mission church teacher-training programs had been systematically destroyed and replaced by an inferior system. Under Bantu education, Black teachers were to be "trained in institutions designated solely for Africans, separate and distinct from the training provided for other sectors of the South African people, under the direct control of segregated education departments, as part of the broader policy of apartheid or separate development" (Hartshorne 1992, pp. 236–237). No training colleges for Blacks were to be established in urban areas, only in the homelands. Teacher-training colleges were to be larger and more economical to operate; a greater proportion of women teachers were to be trained, with an emphasis on preparing elementary teachers. Secondary schools were to be the responsibility of the new Black state universities. By 1968, the Junior Secondary Teachers' Certificate (JSTC) was introduced, requiring a 2-year course that followed senior certification/matriculation, and in 1972, the Primary Teachers' Certificate (PTC) was introduced as a 2-year course. The PTC gave greater emphasis to students' gaining competence in English and Afrikaans and on practice teaching in situations where there were larger class sizes, double sessions, and limited facilities and equipment. In 1977, a Senior Secondary Teachers' Certificate (SSTC) was introduced by adding a 3rd year to the existing 2-year JSCT. Only about 50 student teachers completed this course. According to Hartshorne,

> At best the colleges in the 1970s produced trained craftsmen, but not educated men and women with an understanding of their task, and that of the school, in an increasingly difficult social and political environment. . . . In general it can be said that they were not educated to become autonomous, with a strong concern for both independence and responsibility, but rather to become loyal and obedient employees of the State, who would follow the instructions and regulations of the departments that employed them. (1992, p. 243)

In 1983, the decision was made to upgrade all training colleges to the status of colleges of education and a new 3-year Secondary Teachers' Diploma (STD) was established, which allowed matriculation exemption to entrants who took four degree courses as part of their diploma (which those with senior certificate qualifications did not have to take). The acquisition of this 3-year nongraduate diploma gave the candidates matriculation-exemption status, so that they could proceed to university courses if they wished. The immediate result of this was that almost no secondary school teachers were produced at the end of 1983 because of the lengthening of the course. The same step was taken with the training of primary school teachers, with the old 2-year certification being replaced by a 3-year diploma (PTD). The immediate effect was reduced production of primary teachers. At the beginning of 1988, 17% of Department of Education and Training (DET) primary school teachers and 3.7% of secondary teachers were without any professional qualifications, and only 6,032 new teachers were available to fill 10,338 new positions. Because of the shortages in qualified teachers, homeland institutions created an internship program in which unqualified "national service" teachers could be used in special projects, to release teachers for periods of full-time study and to provide support to schools in particular need. These national-service student teachers remained in contact with the colleges and universities throughout the year to receive distance teaching or an "open university" course of study.

The Normal School Model in the United States

At the dawn of the 20th century, the infrastructure necessary for a viable Black public school system did not exist. Nearly two thirds of Black children of elementary school age were not enrolled in school, primarily because there were not enough school buildings or seating capacity to accommodate the overwhelming majority of these children. Another serious problem was the shortage of Black teachers. Adequate numbers of common schools for Black students could not be developed until there were Black teachers to teach in them, because most southern White teachers would not teach Black students. According to Anderson (1988), a system of second-class education for

Blacks emerged as a logical outgrowth of a social ideology "designed to adjust black southerners to racially qualified forms of political and economic subordination" (p. 3).

In the 1900s, several kinds of schools struggled to control and shape Black teacher training with the assumption that those who shaped the beliefs and behaviors of the teachers would also heavily influence the hearts and minds of Black schoolchildren (see Anderson, 1988, p. 115). One model was the Hampton-Tuskegee normal school, which offered a curriculum of 2 or 3 years in length and did not grant a bachelor's degree. The completion of a 4-year secondary school curriculum was not required for admission to Hampton or other normal schools. Alternatives to the normal school's precollegiate academic program were teachers' college, state, municipal, or incorporated private institutions, or an independent unit of a recognized college or university that had at least one 4-year unified curriculum. These other institutions required a standard 4-year secondary program for admission and granted a standard bachelor's degree. Hampton, by contrast, "was neither a college nor a trade school but a normal school composed of elementary school graduates who were seeking 2 additional years of schooling and teacher preparation courses so that they might qualify for a common school teaching certificate" (Anderson, 1988, p. 35).

Most Black teachers who taught in Black schools attended these normal schools. Their programs placed a strong emphasis on manual labor. The night school program required students to labor 10 hours a day, 6 days a week, 11 months a year. In general, normal school graduates tended to be less well educated, older, and more economically disadvantaged than college students and sought the goal of becoming an elementary school teacher.

In 1900, the largest supply of Black teachers depended on the private normal schools, secondary schools, and colleges. These Black graduates, whether they had received teacher training or not, were filling public-school positions. Still, there was a great need for teachers, and the annual demand for approximately 7,000 new Black teachers was increasing at a much faster rate than the yearly output of about 2,000 Black teachers for the almost 2.5 million Black students aged 5 through 18.

During the 20th century, states began to require a high school diploma for admission to the normal schools. This step automatically put the normal schools on the college level and led to higher academic and professional standards in teacher training. Meanwhile, nearly all the colleges and universities developed teacher-training programs, and soon larger numbers of Black students were going into teaching than into any other postgraduate profession. The development of teacher-training programs for Black students in the South evolved because White school authorities were unwilling to enforce equally high standards for Black students. By World War I, only Virginia, Alabama,

Maryland, and North Carolina maintained Black state normal schools. How-ever, the output from these schools was insufficient to meet local demand, and thus the supply of Black teachers depended almost entirely upon the Black private secondary and normal schools and colleges. By 1932, except for Louisiana, all southern states had abolished teacher-training work in the public Black secondary schools. At this time, approximately 75% of the Black high school teachers in the South had at least a bachelor's degree, and about 9% of the Black elementary school teachers had at least a bachelor's degree.

In the 1954 case, *Brown v. Board of Education*, the United States Su-preme Court ruled that segregation was unconstitutional, overturning the "separate but equal" doctrine of *Plessy v. Ferguson* (1896). The Court en-dorsed the plaintiffs' central thesis that segregation was inherently unequal no matter how much effort the school system claimed to have made to en-sure that Black and White schools had equivalent facilities, staffing, books, buses, and so on. More than 20 years passed, however, before some school districts implemented school desegregation programs. In recent years, racial and ethnic segregation has been on the rise. Orfield, Bachmeier, James, and Eitle (1997) reported that the greatest movement toward resegregation since *Brown v. Board of Education* occurred between 1991 and 1995.

While development of systems of second-class schools and teacher edu-cation programs for Blacks in South Africa and the United States emerged as a logical outgrowth of a social ideology designed to adjust Blacks to ra-cially qualified forms of political and economic subordination, teacher quality has historically been and continues to be one of the most critical factors in determining student achievement, particularly in poor and underresourced schools. In fact, the poorer the community, the greater the effect of school and teacher quality on student achievement.

TEACHER RESPONSES TO THESE COMMON BONDS AND SIMILAR CIRCUMSTANCES

In South Africa and the United States, the goal of consigning Blacks to a subordinate category was most effectively accomplished by limiting and controlling their teachers and ensuring that Black teachers received minimal resources, inadequate training, and limited access to wider knowledge (see Woodson, 1977). In other words, South African and U.S. teachers were sys-tematically deskilled, to keep them from getting too ambitious and to limit their capacity to empower and enlighten their Black student populations. Even today, in schools educating predominantly poor, Black, and marginalized students, teacher qualifications are still an area of concern; for example, most math and science teachers in these schools are still not fully qualified to teach these subjects at advanced levels. Although most teachers in these schools are now professionally qualified to teach basic classes, few have specializations in teaching higher-level mathematics and the sciences (see Howie, 2003), they teach from ragged or outdated textbooks, and they are forced to use a mandated curriculum. Yet they are required to prepare their students for high-stakes examinations that, in addition, are biased in many ways.

In assessing this situation, one might assume that the Black teachers working under these conditions had an attitude of defeat and a low sense of efficacy, pointing to the most apparent sources of their demoralization: poor working conditions, inadequate education and professional training, and the many disruptions that characterized school life in impoverished schools. However, this assumption would be incorrect. A critical factor in the dynamics of education during United States segregation and South African apartheid was the response of teachers to imposed educational policies and conditions. Over the years, their responses were marked by a tension between resistance (to the inferior education that was intended for Blacks) and cooperation (in hopes of attaining better teaching and learning conditions). In the midst of these most demoralizing conditions, Black teachers were by no means completely passive or disempowered. Many, in fact, were organized, strongly progressive leaders in opposition against repressive educational policies and practices.

In the United States, the historical study of Black resistance practices goes as far back as slavery, yielding a compelling vision of slave culture as a set of collective practices that amounted to a system that challenged the absolute control of the master (Faust, 1980). According to Faust, it is a fallacy to view slaves as "passive recipients" of the whims and dictates of their masters. Rather, they actively contested the extent of the slave masters' control, often engaging in subversive practices to undermine the intents of the masters (see Abdullah, Kamberelis, & McGinley, 1992, p. 381). Many of these practices centered around education; some literate slaves secretly taught other slaves to read and write, although this was a punishable offense with severe penalties. Nor were ex-slaves passive recipients of the educational programs offered by missionaries, southern Whites, the Freedmen's Bureau, or northern philanthropists (Anderson, 1988). Rather, they actively resisted the control of their children's education by outside forces. In 1879 Harriet Beecher Stowe said of the freedmen's campaign for education: "They rushed not to the grog-shop but to the schoolroom—they cried for the spelling book for bread, and pleaded for teachers as a necessity of life" (Anderson, 1988, p. 5). Black teachers opened "native schools" throughout the South through self-initiated and self-sustaining efforts; the spirit of these teachers lives on today in African-centered schools, private schools, community-based organizations, and a number of charter schools established for the purpose of providing excellent educational experiences for Black students. In addition, the black church has historically served as a community-based organization where teaching and learning often occurred for African American populations.

In South Africa, for the first 2 decades of Bantu education teachers posed the most organized resistance to state policies. In the 1940s and 1950s, African teachers who had been working in mission or community schools, and who had long been involved in teacher organizations, joined forces with radical liberation groups and African nationalist movements (see Hyslop, 1990). Although underpaid and generally underqualified, these teachers had not previously been servants of the state and they worked hard to promote the interests of African education. Even with the banning and suppression of liberation movements such as the ANC and the Pan-African Congress in the early 1960s and the state crackdowns and educational crisis of the 1970s and 1980s, some South African teachers continued to create alternative curriculum and pedagogy through general activism and various unions and initiatives. In the late 1970s, when the population of African urban secondary schools tripled, a new generation of youth was increasingly exposed to political ideas by individual teachers who had been influenced by the Black-consciousness movement spearheaded by Steven Biko (Hyslop, 1988). Teachers who sided with students who expressed grievances could be suspended, transferred, or dismissed; a small contingency of teachers continued to take that risk. During some of the most repressive times in the education of Black students in both the United States and in South Africa, teachers have been able to find individual spaces in which they could operate in socially and professionally responsible ways, with dignity and a strong sense of teacher efficacy.

This legacy of active resistance, progressive leadership, and the ability to find spaces where they can operate in socially and professionally responsible ways with dignity and a strong sense of efficacy has been a persistent characteristic of successful teachers in schools that have done a good job of educating poor, Black, and marginalized students. With global trends showing youth of color as the world's fastest-growing population group, the schools of the 21st century will have an even greater need for teachers who not only are well trained, but also possess this spirit of resistance, leadership, dignity, and efficacy—teachers who are determined to make a difference in their students' achievement (Armour-Thomas, Clay, Domanico, Bruno, & Allen, 1989; Ferguson, 1991). Despite this need, in the United States underprepared and undercommitted teachers constitute more than 25% of the number hired each year in schools that serve poor, Black, and marginalized students (National Commission on Teaching and America's Future, 1996; NDRC, 1992)—and the percentage is even higher in South Africa (Bhola, 1994; Hartshorne, 1992). The majority of these underprepared teachers in both countries are assigned to schools and classrooms that serve their nation's most vulnerable students—those who are poor, ethnically and linguistically diverse, and at risk of educational failure (Bhola, 1994; Darling-Hammond, 1990, 1992; Hartshorne, 1992; Oakes, 1990). A promising movement in South Africa involves efforts to train and certify "barefoot teachers" who are committed to teaching in impoverished community schools in townships, informal settlements, and rural areas where there are insufficient qualified teachers (Henning, 2000). These unlicensed teachers, who lack official certification, have taught and provided other educational services in rural schools for many years—their pedagogical expertise centers on their knowledge of the community and the students they teach. This phenomenon of barefoot teachers is not limited to the developing world (Darling-Hammond, 1998); globally, these teachers are moving toward professionalization and formal certification.

The fact remains, however, that because of the limited capacities of many uncommitted teachers, most classrooms serving poor, marginalized, and underachieving students continue to provide these students with significantly less engaging and less effective learning experiences (Darling-Hammond, 1995; Dreeben, 1987; Oakes, 1985). Because of the magnitude of this problem and the critical role teachers must play in school reform, it is imperative that we develop a better understanding of the teachers who teach in and the students who attend underresourced schools. One way to increase our understanding of the plight of these students and teachers is by listening to their narratives. Listening to the voices of students and teachers, such as those in the chapter that follows, can give us insight into what is needed to transform underprepared teachers into leaders with the disposition, skills, and sense of efficacy needed to become effective teachers of racially, ethnically, and linguistically diverse student populations.

Parallel Stories, Parallel Dreams: Narratives That Link Lives Across National Boundaries

*Sharing the Voices of U.S. and
South African Students and Teachers*

THE SOUTH AFRICAN and U.S. teachers and students whom I met and worked with from 1994 to 2005 had much in common—and, of course, striking differences as well. The narratives that follow are a starting point for probing the current parallels that have emerged from the social, economic, and political histories described in Chapter 2, and a starting point for global dialogue and cross-national communication. The portraits reveal life experiences in the educational and professional lives of several teachers and in- and out-of-school experiences of a number of students— similar to those that today's teachers are preparing to teach. Common themes emerge in the stories these individuals share, as they talk about their "most memorable learning experiences." These narratives reveal important insights concerning what to them "counts as learning," as well as some of the experiences that have most shaped their lives as learners. These stories serve two functions: They shine a light on the lives and work of students and teachers in economically challenged communities and they help us to understand how learners make sense of their experiences through narrative. By listening to the voices of these individuals, teachers can gain insights from which they can begin to craft a nuanced understanding of the lived experiences of their students, and interested others can gain insights from which to craft expanded visions for changing and restructuring schools and teacher-preparation programs.

SHARING NARRATIVES IN ALTERNATIVE LEARNING ENVIRONMENTS

With the aim of extending the picture that was presented in Chapter 2 and to explore some of the present-day similarities that emerged from the histories discussed there, I used a two-stage methodology to collect the data reported on in this chapter, relying on written reflections and qualitative interviews. This data was collected in nonformal, alternative learning environments where young people had frequent opportunities to recount memories of their learning experiences. In these settings, I collected personal narratives from a broad range of Black learners and their teachers, who varied in age, gender, and educational experience.

In many underresourced communities of the United States and in the townships and rural areas of South Africa, millions of Black youths are not being adequately prepared for successful and immediate transitions into either a world of work or continued academic advancement. Often these underprepared young people are labeled as "marginalized" or as "a lost generation" because of disruptions in their educational experiences, resulting from violence, poverty, or political unrest in their communities. Many turn to community-based organizations and NGOs for alternative learning environments, to escape the narrowly defined channels of traditional, formal schooling that have failed to meet their needs. These alternative learning environments include community-based job training programs, rites-of-passage mentoring programs, and grassroots teacher-training programs that allow young people to share narratives about their personal experiences and the everyday learning that influences their lives.

Community-based organizations and NGOs have become an integral part of an alternative education system in both the United States and South Africa. These programs offer choices to young people who seek another chance on the road to personal, academic, or economic success. The programs range in focus and form, from service programs to commitment and self-concept-building programs; from basic-education and training programs in literacy, technical, and commercial skills to "second chance" or "last chance" programs for those with a wide range of secondary and postsecondary schooling experiences.

I collected narratives of the "most memorable learning experiences" from 100 young people who participated in a range of alternative learning environments established to support marginalized youth and young adults. Fifty were participants in four programs designed to prepare youth and transitioning adults to enter the workplace. Although different in organizational structures, all four programs had the common goal of working to provide job training to marginalized populations—either to men and women who had been denied access to quality education at some level of their schooling or to men and women who, for various reasons, had not taken full advantage of the resources available to them. The four programs were all motivated by the belief that their participants had the potential to make significant contributions to the social, economic, and political stability of their communities. Each program focused on the development of job skills and the creation of employment opportunities for people who had been denied access to traditional routes of upward mobility or had undergone other forms of discrimination. In the United States, 25 participants came from a job-training program in a midwestern inner-city community. In South Africa, 25 participants came from job-training programs located in Johannesburg and Durban.

Also included in my study were 50 students in three programs designed to develop the ethos of service and a commitment to building personal pride in young adults as they prepared to enter the workplace. In the United States, 25 of these participants attended a program that was located in a midwestern inner-city community. It provided a rites-of-passage mentoring program to help African American females prepare for "womanhood" in the tradition of the Xhosa peoples of southern Africa. The remaining 25 participants were South African youth who were involved in nontraditional teacher-training programs that worked to upgrade the qualifications of underprepared teachers or to prepare nondegreed teachers to integrate democratic practices in classrooms where they currently volunteered—programs similar to the one described by Henning (2000).

The 100 participants were composed of 49 males and 51 females who had experienced varying time lapses since leaving formal school environments. Fifty of the participants were African Americans, and 50 were at one time considered Bantu or Black South Africans. Ninety of the participants were students and 10 were teachers. I reported a more detailed account of this research earlier (Ball, 1998b); here, I look specifically at what can be learned from these narratives in regard to the preparation of teachers to teach students from diverse racial, ethnic, and language groups. My findings confirm the value of having teachers of diverse populations (and other interested stakeholders) listen to the voices of their students to gain insights about their lived experiences and perspectives on in- and out-of-school learning (see also Fox, 1992; McEwan & Egan, 1995). As Dyson and Genishi (1994) have noted,

> [Stories] help us to make sense of, evaluate, and integrate the tensions inherent in experience: the past with the present, the fictional with the "real," the official with the unofficial, the personal with the professional, the canonical with the different or unexpected. Stories help us transform the present and shape the future . . . so that it will be richer or better than the past. . . . They help us see possibilities, they give us what we need to envision a transformed future in which learners have satisfying social relationships . . . [and] see themselves in the world around them. (pp. 242–243)

This is the way narrative has been used by the teachers and students in my study. The youth and the teachers who share their voices have found their way to neighborhood learning environments where they are allowed opportunities to make sense of, evaluate, and integrate the tensions in their life experiences.

After an initial period geared toward establishing rapport with them, I approached students and teachers in the South African and U.S. programs and requested individual, and in some cases paired or small-group, interviews to discuss and have them write about their most memorable learning experiences. In addition, I asked each participant, "What do you think you've learned as you look back on these experiences?" As the narratives evolved, I noted that three recurring themes emerged in the recounting of the participants' most memorable learning experiences: (1) experiences related to contexts of violence or personal loss that teach lessons about life; (2) experiences related to institutionalized discipline or corporal punishment that were recalled as vital growth experiences; and (3) experiences that centered around a particular teacher or mentor who was dedicated, supportive, and committed to having high standards of performance and achievement. About 80% of the narratives fell into these three categories, with the remaining 20% grouped in a miscellany of unrelated topics. The narrative excerpts that follow open a window on the conditions under which poor and marginalized youth are expected to learn, offering insights that can be useful to teachers, teacher educators, administrators, and policy makers concerned about preparing teachers for today's schools.

NARRATIVES OF VIOLENCE AND PERSONAL LOSS: LIFE LESSONS

One might expect that a typical response to the request, Tell me about your most memorable learning experience, would relate to a classroom experience or an encounter with an academic subject; many narratives, however, like the one shared by the young African American student below, describe personal danger, weapons in school, and attempted murder. This particular student told of a shocking incident involving violence that ultimately led to her suspension from school:

> My most memorable learning experience was when I got kicked out of Technical Prep High School. I was with some friends one day after school and my friend got into a fight. . . . Crystal pulled out the knife, so I jumped in to take it from her and break up the fight. . . . The next day at school . . . they questioned us; we got kicked out of school for about a month and a half. We got sent to Juvenile for the weekend, it was all messed up. . . . What did I learn in the long run

from that experience? I learned to leave well enough alone, to mind my own business, and when I see someone going to kill somebody else, I'll just let it [happen].

This narrative speaks in the past tense of dynamics that occurred outside the classroom that dramatically influence students' success inside the classroom. For poor African and African American youths, often a context of violence exists within and beyond the academic setting—and it emerges all too often in their narratives as an important element of what they are "learning" about on a daily basis.

Violence in the lives of South African students emerged as a prominent theme in their narratives. Much of the violence they recounted stemmed from the political context in which students, and even teachers, lived. In one narrative, a male teacher and program director recalled how political violence had interrupted the education of many students, to the point that they were unable to pass their matriculation (graduation) examinations. Now the director of a program designed to give a second chance to students who have failed these examinations, this former classroom teacher stated that his own high school education was frequently interrupted as a result of student protests. He recalled:

Many of the male parents would come and look for students who they regarded as ringleaders—students who were leading the campaigns against the government. Those students were identified as ringleaders and then parents would simply come to schools to see those students because they wanted . . . to give them some bashing [beatings].

He ended his narrative by recalling that on more than one occasion he and his friends were chased on their way home from school by a gang of such parents. Others shared stories of domestic violence, such as the student who wrote about an abusive father who would not allow her to keep the lights on late in the evenings when she was trying to complete her homework assignments. She concluded by describing some of the ways she managed to get her assignments completed, such as arriving at school early or working at the home of a friend.

Narratives of personal loss, such as the death or near-death of a loved one (a parent, friend, spouse, or sibling), also emerged as a prominent theme in the students' most memorable learning experiences. When examined within a context of poverty and marginalization, these narratives again illustrate the hostile and violent environments that students must negotiate daily. They also tell of experiences that influence these individuals' identity development. The lessons learned from these narratives are significant because they demonstrate how poor and marginalized young people are painfully aware of their mortality and that of others on whom they depend for support systems. One African American student recounted:

> My most memorable experience is when my mother almost passed away last month. . . . My mother is a 37-year-old Black, young single parent who has Lupus and arthritis, half of a kidney and liver almost gone, and is on dialysis and still working. . . . All I could do was cry and all I could say was, "Well, I didn't get to tell her I was sorry or how much I love her or I need her. And, most of all, please don't leave me. I need you."

This participant noted that the rendering of this narrative motivated her to realize how much she valued her mother after her mother's hospitalization. The sudden and unexpected thought of having to live without her mother moved her deeply; it scared her and taught her a great deal about herself and her present needs.

The teachers who shared their narratives voiced an understanding of how their students felt because of the similar experiences they shared. In her response to the statement, "Tell me about your most memorable learning experience," one U.S. teacher said:

> Losing my husband was my most memorable learning experience. It made me realize that tomorrow is not promised to anyone. . . . It was a long time before I could stop being angry and feeling abandoned. . . . I have to pray to ask God to help me deal with the anger I still have for him not being there to share in the triumphs and trials of raising our daughter. It doesn't seem fair. . . . What did I learn from this experience? I learned that you should live each day as if it were your last and not hesitate to let a person know how much you love and appreciate them. Tomorrow is really promised to no one. . . . I learned this firsthand.

This teacher shifts from the past, to the present, then to the future in describing this turning point in her life. Her narrative builds on a past tragedy to theorize about the realities of the future: *Tomorrow is really promised to no one.* Like the students who have shared their narratives before her, this teacher acknowledges the painful feelings that she must reconcile within herself before she can effectively engage with others in sensitive ways.

NARRATIVES OF DISCIPLINE AND CORPORAL PUNISHMENT

Another major theme that emerged centered on experiences related to institutionalized discipline or corporal punishment. Narratives by both African and African American learners explored a wide range of issues concerning identity development as participants were confronted by institutional conflicts within their environment. These narratives provided insights into the processes by which marginalized individuals come to terms with an environment shaped by a dominant society and institutionalized racism that they feel oppresses them. In their narratives, participants theorized about how they had to learn to deal with hostile or dysfunctional institutions (family, judicial system, political system, educational system). These institutions were often depicted as primary sites in which marginalized young people are socialized into the rules and expectations of society. One U.S. student writes:

> The most memorable learning experience I had was going to [prison].
> . . . They took me from being a first-class citizen to being nobody.
> During the course of my 2½ years . . . I had time to think about
> where I had gone wrong and what I had done. That's how I spent
> most of my time, being analytical. I looked at past situations to see
> how I would approach them differently. . . . I took that negative and
> changed it into a positive. While I was in prison I was placed on work
> detail. That meant I could get the chance to leave the prison and go
> out and work in the community. The majority of the people I worked
> around [were] 99.8% White, which I had never experienced before. I
> heard my language skills become more versatile because after I left
> work I had to go back to prison where the language was in the form
> of street language. I took the time out to read and understand things I
> wouldn't normally look at while I was in the free world. The most
> important thing was I got my values together—more book knowledge
> and more street sense [common sense]. What I learned in the long run
> from the experience was versatility.

Many of these narratives recount pivotal moments in the development of self-perceptions and perceptions about an individuals' relationship to his or her environment or ability to influence that environment. By using his analytical skills, his linguistic versatility, and independent study, this student began to take control over his environment and his future. The following narrative by a South African teacher describes an incident of institutional punishment. This traumatic experience motivated the teacher to become even more committed to what she believed in: the concepts of democracy and educational equity for all.

> I was thrown out of school as a teacher in 1972 because I differed with the White inspector. I criticized the racist School Committee for their interference. Even though I was an excellent teacher, I was blacklisted afterward and had to leave South Africa. Injustice made me fight for justice and the proper running of schools. Wherever I went, I worked diligently to address what I've carried with me, and . . . [to get others to start] looking at representation and participation by legitimate people in the running of education.

Other South African participants described memories of how corporal punishment was administered to students who were late for class, made noise, or gave incorrect responses. Their narratives told of punishments that included beatings or having to scrub the dining-hall floor or chop wood. Other participants recalled having to memorize long recitations in English and in Afrikaans without an understanding of what they were reciting. Several recalled that if students did not know their verses or failed their exams, they were beaten.

Although students no longer receive beatings for being late to school, during my 2004 school visits I observed more than 100 students being locked outside the school gates because they arrived late to a township school. I do not doubt that some of these students were late because of home or community circumstances that were beyond their control. Nevertheless, they were forced to suffer humiliation, required to pick up trash on the school grounds. This is not a practice I observed in the elite schools, although I am certain that some of their students were late to school as well. The narratives shared by poor students tell of experiences that had the long-term effect of teaching them strategies for survival that would allow them to "play in the game" by following the rules. Several participants summarized the realizations that resulted from their confrontations with the system. One wrote:

> Being in jail around other inmates illustrated that I was or had a more intelligent view of life. I saw more opportunities than most of the inmates saw themselves. I knew that I could become a productive part of society, rather than a problem to society.

Another participant summarized his realization this way:

> My most memorable learning experience was when I got incarcerated. I'm sharing this, because to me it's not an embarrassment, it's a learning experience. Before I got incarcerated I really didn't value my freedom. Nor did I realize how short life is. How you live the majority of your life is based on just a couple of ill-used or beneficially used

years. . . . A lot of people don't have the chance to get a break from their families and jobs. To be by themselves and realize, What is my life really about? Am I living for myself or for the people that I am around? In my eyes these people are blind to the facts just like I was. And now for the first time, my eyes are open.

For most of these individuals, interactions with the school system or the criminal justice system were traumatic experiences that taught them that they needed to find alternative routes for participation in society if they hoped to maintain their dignity and freedom. It is ironic that such profound insights were learned in the midst of such circumstances as being incarcerated by a racialized, classist system. It is, however, a long-standing and continuing reality that teachers should be aware of.

NARRATIVES OF INSPIRING TEACHERS

A final theme that emerged from these narratives was that of a particular teacher or mentor who was dedicated, supportive, or committed to high standards of performance and achievement. The narratives described teachers who made learning an enjoyable experience and how students were inspired by them. A common theme that emerged from the narratives of both South African and African American participants was that teachers who encouraged and supported students through positive reinforcement influenced the latter's lives. Among the African American students, one wrote:

One teacher that I will always remember is Mrs. Edna Holmes. . . . She made me feel important. . . . Every time I sit down to read a book I always keep her in mind and try not to forget that she taught me that reading and writing can be lots of fun when you put your mind to it and you work hard at it.

Another student wrote of how encouragement by a teacher contributed to her learning math:

My most memorable experience was with my math teacher in 10th grade—Ms. Smith. Math was always my worst subject [but] Ms. Smith made math fun to learn. She took the necessary time out to teach the kids. If you ever needed individual time or tutoring, she was always available or she gave you a specific time that she could help you. She taught with effectiveness. She was not satisfied unless you were. She constantly stressed the importance of trying and succeeding. She said, more than anything, you should "never say never. You can learn from this." She was one of the best teachers that I came into an encounter with. She made it her business for me to learn.

These narratives defy the widespread myth that poor, underachieving students shun high standards. Rather, they tell of the positive influence teachers had on the developing self-confidence of students and their learning.

All the teachers who shared their narratives voiced an understanding of how their students felt because of similar experiences they themselves had shared. Like their students, these teachers frequently spoke of their own need to negotiate violence or loss before they could engage with the formal educational system. They, too, spoke of the powerful influence of a teacher or mentor who was dedicated, supportive, or committed to high standards of performance in their own lives. Several teachers told me that their teaching practices were inspired by teachers who used positive reinforcement in their early school experiences. A common theme that emerged from the narratives of African and African American youths and their teachers was that teachers who encouraged and supported students through positive reinforcement had a great influence on their students' lives.

These narratives illustrate the fact that caring, committed teachers can affect the lives of young students who are facing various hardships. The encouragement these teachers offered to students boosted students' self-confidence and self-esteem and left a lasting impression on their lives and learning. The students were strongly affected because their teachers had faith in them, in their ability to succeed, and knew how to teach them. The goal of teacher education programs should be to prepare teachers who will motivate, encourage, inspire, and teach. I found it of note that a lower number of students than I had expected wrote narratives about inspiring teachers. We live in a society that demeans, demoralizes, and disrespects teachers; in the media and through public policies, they are depicted as inept. This may have influenced the stories of the students. However, the commentary on teachers who encouraged and supported students through positive reinforcement is a testament to good teachers and gives us confidence that well-prepared, committed teachers can have a lasting influence on students who live very complicated lives.

These narratives by U.S. and South African learners demonstrate the power of stories to call attention to similar themes and common experiences in the educational lives of students and teachers in underresourced communities across national boundaries. As the narratives unfold, it becomes evident that listening to the voices of students and teachers who teach and learn in marginalized areas in these two countries has great potential for revealing important issues about how to teach in distressed environments that should be considered as we prepare teachers to work in challenging schools.

Of particular interest are the narratives that reveal similarities in the lived experiences of teachers and their students. They help us to understand the nature of the informed sensitivity and concern that can be developed by teachers who truly understand the lived experiences of their students because they themselves have succeeded in spite of the situations they have endured. This informed sensitivity and concern can contribute to a teacher's developing sense of efficacy and belief in the capabilities of their students.

THE VALUE OF SHARING CRITICAL MOMENTS

The narratives quoted earlier give a glimpse into the lives of poor and marginalized learners and their teachers, helping us to understand human experiences within a global context. They also illustrate Hans Gadamer's (1976) notion that our past influences us in everything we want, hope for, or fear in the future, and only as we are possessed by our past are we opened to the new, the different, and the true. If we accept Gadamer's theory, then it follows that learning for the "self" takes place through the lenses of past learning experiences: that human lives are continuing narratives and developing stories.

For both African and U.S. participants, one primary value of recounting most memorable learning experiences through narratives centered on the importance of giving these individuals opportunities to reflect upon critical moments in their lives that they may not have had in the past. In recounting their experiences, the participants were given an opportunity to gain new understandings from the events. Students most often exhibited an ability to make connections between specific remembered learning events and changes that took place in their prior behaviors or value systems. In many cases, remembered experiences, particularly those that involved death, violence, or serious trauma, were life-changing events that altered the narrators' perspective on their lives and the world around them. The initial influence of the event may have been one of discouragement, hurt, or sadness. Being presented with the occasion to "tell me about your most memorable learning experience," however, provided these storytellers with an opportunity to retell, to relive, and perhaps to reenvision, these experiences. But they were now telling or living the experience within the safe, nonjudgmental context of a relationship that had been established with a sympathetic listener. Considering these experiences within a supportive context provided an opportunity for the students and teachers to confront the situations anew. In this context, the mere asking of the question was an empowering experience, as each participant voiced a realization that little genuine interest had ever been shown by a researcher or interested other concerning their learning experiences or how they viewed the world.

Students and teachers repeatedly admitted that if they had been asked to comment on these experiences while they were actually going through them, they would probably have simply reported on their frustrations, their feelings of helplessness, and their desire to remove themselves from the situation or abandon the project at hand. Having reflected as a result of this study, and having the distance in time since the incidents actually occurred, allowed each one an opportunity to consider the experiences anew, as life-teaching lessons or as vital experiences for growth. With the passing of time and the mellowing effects of retrospect, these participants were able to come to a reflective stance in which they were able to use the narrative reports as heuristic opportunities. They could come to a realization of the value and growth potential that developed as a result of the experience.

Perhaps through our engagement with the stories of those who teach and learn in inner-city or underresourced environments, we can come to better understand their qualities of resilience and ability to see the good even in difficult circumstances. Engaging with the narratives of these students and teachers can help us to gain a clearer understanding of their worlds and the resources they bring to the learning experience and can lead to a clearer understanding of how to prepare teachers to work with these students.

Bruner (1994) takes a constructivist view of narrative and proposes that "world making" is the principal function of the mind and that people use narrative to interpret and reinterpret their experiences. He further proposes that we tell stories the way we see life:

> I believe that the ways of telling and the ways of conceptualizing that go with them become so habitual that they finally become recipes for structuring experience itself, for laying down routes into memory, for not only guiding the life narrative up to the present, but for directing it into the future. I have argued that a life as led is inseparable from a life as told. . . . If we can learn how people put their narratives together when they tell stories from life, considering as well how they might have proceeded, we might then have contributed something new to that great ideal [that is, to the making of a better world]. (pp. 28, 36, 37)

According to Bruner, the students and teachers in my research have shared narratives that tell of the lives they have lived, they have shared insights about how they see life, and they have laid down some of the routes into their memories. If we, as listeners, can gain a better understanding of their life narratives up to the present, perhaps we can become a positive force in directions and possibilities for the future. My hope and belief is that teachers, teacher educators, administrators, and policy makers will listen more sensitively to the stories shared by the students and teachers who live and work in poverty and, moreover, that we will exploit the power of these stories for bringing the diverse experiences of our students into the classroom and into our lives for forging new connections between teachers and students who come from culturally and linguistically diverse backgrounds.

There are pedagogical implications of listening to the narrative voices of students attending poor and underresourced schools. While the Black students and teachers in my study have shared narratives of violence, loss, discipline, incarceration, and dedicated teachers, they have also shared messages about practices and particular teachers that enabled them to see themselves and the world in different ways. The following practices were cited by students and teachers as enabling, and the practices could be woven in as core goals for any lesson. Students said they were enabled to see other perspectives through individualized class attention, extra classes, or working groups held during lunch or after school. They were enabled to see new possibilities for their lives by teachers who provided extra resources and were friendly, nurturing, available, encouraging, or even well prepared for teaching, teachers who used practical examples that related to the students' home or community experiences, teachers who used project-based learning or active learning. Additionally, they were enabled by teachers who cared enough to give homework, those who incorporated the students' home language into their teaching, and those who persisted in holding high standards in a kind and loving way.

Schultz (2003) has noted that listening to students is essential to teaching. She proposes that if we are to educate students to participate in a pluralistic democracy, teachers must listen, to know individual students; listen to the rhythm and balance of the class; listen for the social, cultural, and community context of students' lives; and listen for silence and acts of silencing (p. 2). My research confirms that by listening to the narrative voices of their students, teachers can learn that poor and marginalized young people are painfully aware of their mortality and the mortality of others they depend on to provide support systems in their lives; that some students who have been incarcerated are very articulate about how to take the time to read and understand and look at past situations and use that information as a stepping stone to contemplate a better future; that students who have had traumatic experiences are sometimes motivated to become even more committed to what they believed in; and that for many students interactions with the school system or the criminal justice system have been negative experiences, but, on some occasions, these negative experiences have taught them that they needed to find alternative routes for participation in society if they hoped to maintain their dignity and their freedom. Many successful teachers in these schools voiced an understanding of how their students felt because of the similar experiences they shared. As developing teachers listen to the narrative voices of students attending underresourced schools, they can learn how students feel about their capacities to contribute to their own learning. Through listening, teachers can hear students saying that they *do* have the capabilities and the desire to contribute positively to their own academic success and to the success of others. As one participant put it:

> I can recall participating in the school choir, debate society, and being elected a student representative. Although I did not want to be labeled as intelligent, students realized that I was and asked me to teach them subjects in a study group when our schooling was interrupted. . . . So I began tutoring a group of students. I really thought I was going to fail . . . but along with seven of the eight members of our study group, I passed the exam.

As developing teachers listen to the narrative voices of those living and working in impoverished or underresourced schools, they can come to hear about the characteristics that this population considers important in an effective teacher. Another participant said:

> I had two teachers in Standard 9 and 10 that stood out in my memory because they were not just concentrating on teaching us what was in the textbook but they were also advisors, telling us what is good and what is wrong. . . . But they were not prescriptive, they were not prescribing to us what it is that we ought to do. They were telling us that if we want to live successfully . . . this is what we need to do: We need to be honest with ourselves, we need to respect other people. So they were not just merely teaching what was in the textbook, but their perception of education was much broader than what the textbook was giving. . . . These teachers lived in my community, and they encouraged me outside of school as well.

As developing teachers who are preparing to teach students from diverse racial, ethnic, and language groups listen to the narrative voices of students living in poverty, they can begin to hear what the students are saying about how they want their education to challenge them to become critical thinkers. As one student put it:

> My most memorable educational experience was the influence of my
> Standard 10 English teacher. I remember that when she was teaching
> *Romeo and Juliet* she used different types of outside materials like
> tapes and extra books to help us to understand the story. In her
> teaching, she stressed the act of thinking deeply and critically before
> answering a question or making a comment. . . . And so this teacher
> really stands out in my mind.

And finally, as developing teachers who are preparing to teach students
from diverse racial, ethnic, and language groups listen to the narrative voices
of students living in poverty, they can begin to hear their aspirations. One
student who attended an African-centered rites-of-passage program in the
United States was positively influenced by the female mentors around her.
She used the metaphor of a tulip bud to confidently yet poetically express
her future aspirations for success. She noted that "when given the opportunity, [she] will blossom." This student talked about how she learned so much
by attending an African American student-centered conference.

> Like the tulips, I am searching for the chance to bloom. I aspire to
> blossom into a corporate attorney with a PhD in English. I plan to
> pursue a career in law because I enjoy using my interpersonal com-
> munication and analytical skills. . . . Like the tulip buds, I'm search-
> ing for the right time and place to blossom. When put in the perfect
> crystal vase, I brighten the darkest room.

The narratives shared in this chapter can help prevent the breakdowns
in communication that can occur when teachers who work in underresourced
schools lack familiarity with the students they are trying to teach. Because
of the gulf in experiences between underprepared teachers and students in
underresourced schools, misunderstandings can occur. However, as we listen to our students and consider issues of educational reform, the primary
questions we should be asking are, What do we need to know in order to do
a better job of teaching racially, culturally, and linguistically diverse students,
and what do we need to know in order to do a better job of preparing teachers
to teach students from backgrounds that differ from their own? It is within
this context that we ought to consider the words of Noguera (1995), who
states that when teachers and administrators—and, might I add, teacher
educators and policy makers—remain unfamiliar with the places and the ways
in which their students live their lives outside the school walls, they often fill
this knowledge void with stereotypes based on what they read or see in the
media, and thus fear invariably influences their interactions. In such cases,
listening to the narrative voices of our students can be a powerful tool for

improving understanding, voiding stereotypes, reducing fear, and increasing familiarity with students' lived experiences outside school. Connelly and Clandinin (1990) note that in understanding ourselves and our students educationally, we need an understanding of their life's narratives that are the context for making meaning of school situations. From the sample of narratives presented here, we can learn a great deal about important factors and influences that affect the lives of students both inside and outside school.

The most important point that we should take away from these narratives is that those teachers who continue to be mostly White, monolingual, and monocultural—and who hope to become effective teachers of diverse students—must listen to their students' narratives and participate in their life experiences. Through continued listening, interested others can learn more about the perspectives from which students view the world. Such information can enable us to be more effective as educators who are capable of connecting with our students at meaningful levels. While theorists such as hooks, Freire, Stock, and Bakhtin have alluded to these points, the data presented in this chapter adds new insights and concrete present-day examples that support that theory. Once we are motivated to create narrative spaces in which the sharing of knowledge flows freely, then students, teachers, teacher educators, administrators, and policy makers can become engaged in conversations that lead to teaching and learning activities that allow us to move beyond our past to envision a better future.

WHAT WE KNOW AND WHAT WE NEED TO KNOW

The information provided in this chapter can help us to address the challenge of preparing teachers who have the attitudes, knowledge, skills, and dispositions necessary to work effectively with students from diverse racial, ethnic, and language groups. By listening to the voices of these individuals, teachers can gain insights from which they can begin to craft a nuanced understanding of the lived experiences of their students, and interested others can gain insights from which to craft expanded visions for changing and restructuring schools and teacher-preparation programs. This is critically important because as we enter a new millennium, culturally and linguistically diverse students across the globe are seeking access to quality educational opportunities. These students are becoming increasingly different in background and culture from one another and from their teachers, and an increasing number are poor and marginalized socially and educationally. In many nations, including the United States and South Africa, teachers are asked to teach students who have life experiences that are very different from their own; consequently, today's teaching requires intercultural understanding, personal commitment, and the ability to communicate across cultures, languages, and dialects.

With today's rapidly changing demographics, it is becoming apparent that few teachers are adequately prepared to work effectively with students from culturally and linguistically diverse backgrounds and with students who are socially and economically disenfranchised. Even in South Africa, where most teachers who teach in the poorest schools are teaching in schools attended predominantly by students of color, few teachers are adequately prepared to work effectively with their students, because the students in these classrooms frequently come from different language groups and socioeconomic backgrounds. Most of the Black students in these classrooms are taught by Black teachers; however, because of the apartheid system of undereducating Black teachers, many of these teachers are academically underqualified (Hartshorne, 1992, p. 236). So while most of these teachers may be quite familiar with the cultural backgrounds of their students, they are in the position of having to work in underresourced school environments, teach students whose home languages may differ from their own, and work with students who come from socioeconomic backgrounds that differ from their own.

And so, despite the more frequent instances of cultural congruity between teacher and students, they still have high drop-out rates. This means that teacher education programs will need to not only address the challenge of preparing teachers to work with students from diverse racial, culture, socioeconomic, and linguistic backgrounds, but also focus specifically on addressing the need for an adequate supply and equal distribution of qualified teachers to serve all students. Thus, my call throughout this book is for educational reformers to address this challenge. Accomplishing this goal will require a higher level of commitment on the part of policy makers, administrators, teacher educators, and teachers than currently exists. In addition, we will need ongoing research that focuses on (1) instilling positive attitudes in teachers toward diversity; (2) understanding the processes of teacher change so we can use this information in helping teachers develop the skills and dispositions needed to teach students from diverse backgrounds; and (3) understanding the kinds of activities that need to occur in the teacher education programs to significantly develop teachers' commitment to working in poverty schools with students of color. This research must investigate how teachers move from simply being teachers committed to teaching to become individuals empowered with a strong sense of teacher efficacy and a vision of what it means to be committed to teaching *all* students.

These challenges cannot be met unless we give serious consideration to theoretical frameworks that can undergird our work and help us to better understand how teachers develop an interest in and a commitment to becoming effective teachers of all students. Sociocultural theory, first outlined by Vygotsky (1962, 1978) and further elaborated by Leont'ev (1981) and Wertsch (1991), can provide such a framework. The starting point for the organization of such research must be a theoretical framework that views teachers' conceptual and ideological change as social processes, and it must lend itself to addressing a number of critical questions:

1. How can we restructure teacher education programs to successfully motivate teachers to become interested in acquiring the attitudes, knowledge, skills and dispositions necessary to work effectively with student populations who are different from themselves?
2. How can we structure teacher education programs to foster teachers' interest in understanding the historical, cultural, political, and economic circumstances and resources that students from diverse racial, ethnic, and language groups bring to the classroom?
3. How can we present theory in teacher education programs so that it begins to affect classroom practices?
4. How can we empower teachers to develop their own voices on issues of diversity and become change agents in our schools?

Too often in my career as a teacher educator, I have observed cases in which student teachers were able to produce seemingly appropriate answers to examination questions and class assignments without actually integrating sound theoretical perspectives into their own personal experiences in ways that would allow the power of those perspectives to transform their day-to-day teaching practice. In both the United States and South Africa I encountered students in teacher education programs who were interested in teaching students much like themselves, but who ultimately decided not to engage in teaching students who were poor, underachieving, and attending underresourced schools. I can still recall the look on the face of one student teacher whom I met in my early years as a teacher educator. She said: "I can discuss topics of interest in my undergraduate teacher education classroom and never think about it again until another education class brings up the topic. . . . The knowledge in my brain is doing no good because I'm not using it. . . . Teacher education programs can't force any student to internalize the theories that they have 'learned' in their class." After sensing this same attitude of disinterest from too many students over the period of several years, I wanted to become more proactive in addressing this phenomenon. I began to study my teaching and my students' development, and I developed a course that helped some teachers develop the attitudes, skills, and dispositions necessary to become *change agents* in schools. My teaching approach was guided by a desire to discover the process through which teachers move beyond positions of cognitive internalization of theory and best practices toward transformative positions of reflective commitment. Through a process of teacher change, teachers developed a sense of efficacy and a sense of commitment that guided them in their generative development as effective classroom teachers of diverse students.

Next, in Chapter 4, I present a model that helps to explain that process of teacher change, and, in Chapters 5 to 8, I use the voices of South African and U.S. teachers to demonstrate that process. Through rich examples from the writings of teachers, I demonstrate how that *process of teacher change* took place in the lives of individual teachers and I explore how teachers' developing commitment can be facilitated by a carefully designed teacher education course. I also show how those developing commitments are revealed in the changing discourses and practices of teachers. Through the journal entries, reflective essays, and narratives of teachers, you will share in their personal and professional journeys of transformation toward advocacy and becoming carriers of the torch. Sharing the various texts created *over time* by the teachers opens a window on the developmental processes that were taking place in these teachers' minds, leading to a clearer understanding of how some teachers engaged in that process of change, while others did not.

Cultivating Contemplation on Commitment: Sociocultural Perspectives

The Theoretical Framework That Guides This Research

H ER NAME WAS Melanie, and she attended a teacher education program at a major college in a city in Guatang province, South Africa. In
describing her early literacy experiences, she wrote, "I was exposed to reading and writing at an early age. As far as I can remember, I was able to read
before I could go to school. My mom would always read to me and then I
would read it back to her. . . . I always read classical books [and] my mom
read me fairy tales. This helped to develop my imagination." Melanie thoughtfully recollected, "I had always wanted to be a teacher, ever since I was young
. . . but my parents wanted me to be a lawyer. I started here at the university
studying law, but within 3 to 4 weeks I changed to education. I also studied
some through distance education at UNISA." Melanie was motivated to enter
teacher education in part by her pleasurable memories of her own schooling, but now, as she was completing her 3rd year at the local College of Education, she was having second thoughts. She had deeply contemplated the
idea of a career in education and had often imagined the type of teacher she
would be and the students she wanted to teach.

Melanie began the teacher education program with much enthusiasm,
but her thoughts were beginning to change, and now I could see that she
approached many of her classroom assignments half-heartedly. During one
of our freewrite sessions she explained that she was frustrated by the challenges facing teachers in their increasingly diverse classrooms. She noted that
"teachers are unprepared for the classrooms they are entering." Workers who
had been employed in the cities for some time as domestic workers and laborers, were now bringing their children and grandchildren from the townships to attend the city schools. Some students traveled long distances on foot
or by bicycle to attend schools that had not been available to them during
apartheid. Others came to the historically White city schools from nearby
communities referred to as "informal settlements." Many of these newly
arriving students spoke languages other than the academic English spoken
in the schools, and they came from cultural and socioeconomic backgrounds

that differed from those of their teachers. The limitations facing teachers were exacerbated by the fact that the new curriculum had not been well received.

Melanie was very aware of the limitations teachers faced, and she was frustrated by the constraints she felt would be imposed on her as a teacher. She felt it was unlikely that she would be able to structure her future classroom and her curriculum as she wished. As a result, she had recently made a decision, which she had entered in her journal. As she put it, she had decided:

> This will not work for me. . . . Education in my country is changing at such a rate and has changed very much from when I was a young student at school. If I were to be honest with myself, I know that I do not want to be a teacher for the rest of my life. . . . Since the beginning of this year I've decided I do not want to teach anymore.

Melanie explained that as South African classrooms became increasingly diverse she had begun to question her commitment to teaching. So drastic had been the changes in the educational system in South Africa that many preservice teachers, like Melanie, had decided to abandon teaching as a career. Melanie explained that she was leaving teaching because of the poor preservice training she had received in preparation for the emerging challenges that teachers were facing and because she felt the job provided too few rewards in relation to its responsibilities.

It was teachers like Melanie in my classes who motivated me to start investigating the process of teacher change in a serious way. I was perplexed by the thought that Melanie could spend 3 years in a teacher education program and yet ultimately decide that she did not want to teach. I wondered if through research I could find ways to reignite her commitment to teaching, in general, and, in particular, her interest in teaching students from diverse racial, ethnic, and language groups.

Dingani's story was different from Melanie's, but I found it just as bewildering. Dingani came from a home with few books and experienced reading as a tedious and difficult task in his primary school years, because of the instructional emphasis on memorization and choral reading. While in secondary school, he reported, "I started reading African literature, especially the books written by Ngugi wa Thiong'o, Chinua Achebe, and others. I also read books on the South African [social and political] situation, though it was a risk because some of these books were banned. This reading motivated me."

Despite Dingani's attending an underresourced school and having had unpleasant experiences with reading in his primary years, he developed an interest in reading and writing at his secondary school. These skills supported him in his language and literacy development. After reading about Vygotsky and other education theorists in our class, Dingani reflected,

> Vygotsky (1981) and Cummins (1994) highlight a very crucial issue which has been neglected in Department of Education and Training (DET) schools [schools designated for Black South Africans during apartheid]: that critical literacy and knowledge are attained as a result of interaction between adults and students and that this interaction is very important for the development of literacy. Hudelson (1994) proposed strategies for second-language literacy development. I have learned that teachers must create environments that are conducive to learning and that educators must create a literate classroom environment that will instill confidence in all pupils and that collaborative learning can help bring about real learning in our schools.

Dingani was struck by the notion that teachers must have strong personal relationships with their students. He was also deeply impressed with the concepts of critical literacy and collaboration as useful mechanisms for improving the educational plight of students of color. He shared his changing perspectives on the importance of critical literacy, which requires an individual to apply his or her literacy learning in meaningful ways both inside and outside of schools:

> In my view, literacy now means the ability to read *purposefully* and with understanding, to read the text *and* read between the lines. This will enable the learner to exploit the resources around him [or her] to formulate constructive alternatives. In my opinion, literacy has to produce critical thinkers and creative citizens. Literacy must be offering something worthwhile. . . . Literacy is something that needs to be shared to help others develop personally, socially, intellectually, and otherwise.

Dingani had embraced a critical perspective on literacy in which the members of a truly literate citizenry are responsible for using their literacy in purposeful ways that benefit others in the community—personally, socially, and intellectually. In his final journal entry, Dingani reflected on the class as a worthwhile educational experience and linked it to his emerging philosophy on literacy.

It appears that Dingani felt he had benefited from this course. His perspectives on literacy had broadened in ways that would help him become a successful teacher of students from culturally and linguistically diverse backgrounds. However, with the end of apartheid, Dingani now felt that for the first time in his life, he had choices available to him. No longer was he limited to the career choices of becoming a minister, a common laborer, or a teacher. With the new options that had opened up, he had decided to use his teaching degree as a "steppingstone" to becoming a lawyer, entrepreneur, or corporate executive. Dingani demonstrates how outstanding students of color in our universities are choosing to enter professions other than teaching: We are losing many of our potentially most promising practitioners to other fields that are perceived as being more lucrative and more prestigious.

Through my experiences with students such as Melanie and Dingani, it became apparent to me that one of the greatest challenges facing teacher education programs globally was the need to help teachers acquire the attitudes, skills, disposition, and desire needed to teach all students, particularly those from culturally and linguistically diverse backgrounds. Yet in our teacher education programs we continue to encounter students like Melanie, who have chosen not to enter teaching because of the increased challenges of diversity in the classroom, and like Dingani, who would make excellent teachers but have decided to enter other, more lucrative and prestigious professions. These highly qualified individuals could potentially represent a large proportion of our current and future teaching force. Teacher education programs are challenged to facilitate a change in the attitudes of these potentially outstanding teachers. In addition, I am personally challenged to recruit those who already know that they want to become teachers *and* those who have not yet seriously considered the rewards and challenges of teaching students from diverse backgrounds. I want to inspire those teachers to consider such an option and to develop a commitment to do so.

These challenges motivated me to develop a study that would engage preservice and in-service teachers with theory and strategically selected activities designed to enable them to move from simply being teachers committed to teaching, to become individuals empowered with a vision of what it means to be committed to teaching *all* students. Through this study of the South African and U.S. teachers who participated in my courses, I learned more about the possibilities for facilitating teacher change and the processes that developing teachers go through to become reflective, committed practitioners who are interested in teaching diverse student populations. I also learned some things about the teachers I was unable to engage in this process of change.

THE STUDY

The study that I developed was based on the works of Vygotsky (1978), Wertsch (1991), Wertsch and Stone (1985), Bakhtin (1981), and Leont'ev (1981). Understanding the contributions of these scholars can increase our understanding of the processes of teacher change as they relate to issues of preparing teachers for diversity. Their contributions can also help us design the types of activities that need to occur in teacher education programs to facilitate the development of teachers who are interested in working with societies' fastest-growing populations.

According to Wertsch (1985), three themes underlie a Vygotskian theoretical perspective. First, an individual's internal activity can be understood as it is situated in a broader social and historical context. This notion seems especially important when considering the development of teachers' individual philosophies concerning their work with disenfranchised students within the context of a social system that historically denied access and quality education to students from diverse racial, ethnic, and linguistic groups.

Second, learning is facilitated through the assistance of more knowledgeable members in the community; further, optimum development occurs within the zone of proximal development. For Vygotsky, the zone of proximal development (ZPD) is the distance between the actual level of the individual's development and the level of potential development as determined through problem solving under the influence or guidance of "more informed others" (Vygotsky, 1978, p. 86), who can include a course instructor or peers. Guidance can also be obtained through engagement with more advanced theoretical considerations that serve to enlighten or extend an individual's understanding. By extension, the development of teachers' philosophies on diversity can be altered by engagement with challenging classroom discussions with peers that cause them to question their previously held notions concerning diversity or by contact with more advanced theoretical perspectives presented to them within an individual's zone of proximal development. This also means that teachers' perspectives can change through engagement with the problem-solving activities required when contemplating a teacher research project, when supported by more informed others, and when negotiated within the context of reflective journal writing and discussions that extend and expand the teachers' zones of proximal development.

Third, human action is mediated by signs and tools—primarily psychological signs and tools such as language. The strategic use of oral and written language within our classroom is the predominant means by which we make sense of new theoretical perspectives and give personal meaning to the best practices we engage with. In my work with developing teachers, written reflections and oral discussions have served a meaning-making function as teachers used these mediums to think deeply about their developing philosophies on diversity. Two additional notions grow out of sociocultural theory that can help us understand how a teacher experiences conceptual and ideological change: One is the notion of "ideological becoming" and the other is referred to as "internalization."

Ideological Becoming

In Bakhtin's writings, *ideological becoming* refers to the process of how we come to see the world. Acording to Ball and Freedman (2004):

> In Bakhtinian writings "ideological becoming" refers to how we develop our way of viewing the world, our system of ideas, what Bakhtin calls an ideological self. Although the Bakhtinian school's concept of ideological becoming does not necessarily have a political edge, it does not exclude the development of a political idea system as part of ideological development. (p. 5)

For Bakhtin (1981), the coming together of new perspectives, new ideas, and new voices (represented in the new theoretical perspectives presented to teachers in my course) are essential to a person's growth. The discourses of others can enter our consciousness as authoritative discourses or as alternatives to the ones we once held or currently hold. Thus, the discourses of others can influence the way we think and can contribute to forming what ultimately becomes internally persuasive discourses for us—thus influencing our ideologies—our thoughts, beliefs, and ways of theorizing about a body of ideas, their origin, and how they operate. This process of ideological becoming is critically important to the development of teachers' thinking on issues of diversity because it is through this process that teachers can begin to step out on their own ideologically—through this process they can develop the ability to stand in their classrooms with confidence, with a sense of ownership, and with a sense of personal efficacy when teaching culturally and linguistically diverse students. Presenting teachers with new ideas, theories, and practices in teacher education courses and challenging them to question their preconceived ideas can produce new and independent thoughts, which are needed to bring different perspectives to teaching students from diverse racial, ethnic, and language groups. It is through this process that generative thinking emerges on the part of teachers.

The research reported in this book is based on the notion that ideological becoming can and should occur within the context of teacher education programs that hope to prepare teachers to teach racially, ethnically, and linguistically diverse students. While there is research that documents the prevailing phenomenon of teachers' beliefs being resistant to change (Cohen 1990), Tharp and Gallimore (1988); Richardson (1994); and Harste, Leland, Schmidt, Vasquez, and Ociepka (2004) all support the notion that teachers' perspectives can and do change. They have provided sufficient rationale for the work I conducted concerning the possibilities for teacher change. The work of these researchers has led me to believe that change is not only possible but mandatory in teacher education programs that hope to prepare teachers to work with diverse students in social contexts in which the prevailing norm has been one that devalued the cultural and linguistic resources that particular groups brought to the classroom. And the work of Freeman (1992, 1996) bolstered my prediction that these changes would be reflected in the teachers' emerging discourses.

Building on the assumption that teachers' developing ideologies can be affected by carefully selected course readings and strategically designed course experiences, I exposed the teachers in my course to such readings and activities. For example, teachers in my course read Henry Giroux's (1988), "Teachers as Transformative Intellectuals," a chapter in his *Teachers as Intellectuals*. Giroux proposes that teacher education programs need to be developed to help prospective teachers become transformative intellectuals who are able to affirm and practice the discourse of freedom and democracy. He discusses intersecting fields of struggle that define the nature of teachers' work and the purpose of schooling. He challenges teacher education programs to consider issues of how educators can create a language that enables teachers to consider the role that schooling plays in joining knowledge and power. He encourages them to explore how a radicalized teaching force can provide both empowering teachers and teaching for empowerment. Giroux criticizes most teacher education programs because they neglect to deal with questions concerning the nature of power, ideology, and culture. Although his ideas were published almost 20 years ago, the need to address these issues in teacher education programs remains. In my courses, through much discussion of Giroux's ideas and the ideas of others, teachers came to consider which, if any, of these ideas would become a part of their own discourses. Through this process, teachers began the initial stages of developing their own voices on issues related to preparing teachers to work with students from culturally and linguistically diverse backgrounds.

Internalization

Internalization is a concept that emerges from sociocultural theory, which holds that learning and development occur on two planes (see Wertsch, 1985, p. 163). They first appear on a social plane, occurring between people as an interpsychological category; they then appear on an internal, psychological plane, occurring within an individual as an intrapsychological category. For Vygotsky, internalization is the social process in which an external social activity (such as engaging with theoretical concepts and with best practices on diversity in a class) becomes an internal individual activity or plane of consciousness (for example, taking personal ownership of the concepts or developing a personal commitment to act on concepts).

Vygotsky explains this process of learning and developing through the metaphor of "buds" and "flowers" that, with assistance, will "fruit" into independent accomplishments (1978, p. 86). These "buds" and "flowers" can blossom into efficacious teaching within diverse classrooms. Vygotsky's discussion of internalization can help us to understand how this learning and development occur—how the information presented to teachers in teacher education programs can move from an interpsychological plane as a social exchange in which teacher educators encourage students to consider conceptual innovations, to an intrapsychological plane where these social classroom activities are embraced by teachers to become an internal catalyst that generates teacher advocacy, efficacy, and commitment.

Vygotsky's study of the process called internalization was based largely on an analysis of semantic mechanisms, especially language, that reveal social and individual functioning. Vygotsky's accounts of semiotic mechanisms (or language tools for meaning making) "provided a bridge that connected the external with the internal and the social with the individual" (Wertsch, 1985, p. 164), and this was also the case with my own research. My accounts of the oral and written language that the teachers produced for me throughout the course provided me with a bridge to understanding their process of change—the process of our external curricular exchanges becoming concepts that they personally embraced. The changing discourses of these teachers revealed their movement beyond surface-level engagements with theory toward transformative engagements that led them to take positions of reflective commitment that guided them in their efforts to become more effective teachers of our schools' most vulnerable learners.

Internalization on the part of these developing teachers involved the development of a personal voice on issues related to the teaching and learning of diverse students. *Voice* pertains to the role of language in constructing meaning—it applies to written as well as spoken language and relates to point of view: "It is concerned with the broader issues of a speaking subject's perspective, conceptual horizon, intention and world view" (Wertsch, 1991, p. 51). When internalization is taking place, the personal voices of teachers will begin to emerge, that is, voices that are *their own*. When teachers begin taking the words of theory and recommended best practices and begin transforming those words and practices and adapting them to make them their own, we know that internalization is taking place.

THE COURSE

The primary question that guided my exploratory study was, "What do we need to know in order to do a better job of preparing teachers to teach *all* students effectively, particularly students from diverse racial, ethnic, and language groups?" The following questions were the starting point for my cross-national exploratory study:

1. How can we structure teacher education programs to successfully motivate teachers to become interested in acquiring the attitudes, knowledge, skills, and dispositions necessary to work effectively with student populations who are different from themselves?
2. Can we present theory in teacher education programs so that it begins to effect classroom practices?
3. How can we empower teachers to develop their own voices on issues of diversity and become change agents in our schools?

I designed a course that I taught to South African and U.S. teachers through which I investigated these questions. The course was based on a model that will be described later in this chapter and that was informed by the work of Vygotsky, Bakhtin, Leont'ev, and Wertsch. I designed this course with the specific intentions of investigating the possibility of strategically planning activities that nurture and facilitate the development of teachers who have an increased sense of efficacy and a commitment to teaching students from diverse racial, ethnic, and language groups. The purpose of the course was to familiarize prospective teachers with ways in which reading, writing, and multiple literacies can function in multilingual and multicultural classrooms. The general and specific topics on literacy that students encountered in this course were chosen to help classroom teachers consider how they might want to use multiliteracies to teach their subject matter to diverse student populations. The course raised a number of questions and issues regarding theory and practical strategies for teaching and learning literacy, motivated by an integration of teachers' own teaching/learning/observational experiences with the readings and assignments they did for the course.

The issues that developing teachers examined in the course included (a) What does it mean for people to be literate in our changing society? (b) What values, meanings, and implications does literacy have for people within and outside of school settings? (c) How is literacy and its practices organized within particular classrooms and what effects do these practices have on the way we come to know the world within schools and within particular disciplines? and (d) How can reading and writing be used by teachers to teach their subject matter effectively? At the beginning of the class, we noted that few good questions are answered in the course of one term. Rather, the goal of the course was to open new dialogue and to discover that not only answers but also new questions and issues would emerge as the student teachers studied and taught. We also noted that during their teaching, they would deepen those dialogues and continue the conversation throughout their careers.

Under old paradigms of instruction, preservice and in-service teachers had been given extensive training on lower-level "what to do on Monday morning" types of activities. Seldom were they exposed to the knowledge needed to facilitate classroom learning for diverse students. Many teachers are only prepared to select materials that reflect the dominant culture and societal views and to make curricular and pedagogical choices that manifest their own backgrounds, education, and experiences. What was needed was the expansion of what we define as basic education for preservice and in-service teachers by opening up the curriculum to a variety of perspectives and experiences; by exposing teachers to complex theoretical ideas that require them to use critical thinking, reasoning, and problem solving; and by charting new directions for instruction. We know that this is possible because Harste and colleagues (2004) tracked four teachers during their preservice program and 2 years later and found that theoretical perspectives initially acquired in their teacher education programs strongly influenced their curriculum and instruction choices and whether they perceived themselves as change agents.

To engage the teachers in my course in interpersonal and intrapersonal conversations about becoming change agents—conversations that would require them to use critical thinking, reasoning, and problem solving to think about charting new directions for instruction—I drew on the work of Bakhtin (1981) and Gee (1989). This scholarship helped them build a theoretical framework that would support them in their future work. Three key concepts underscore Bakhtin's beliefs about semiotic mediation: dialogicality, voice, and utterance (Wertsch, 1991). Dialogicality is one central notion in Bakhtin's work. It refers to "the ways in which one speaker's concrete utterances come into contact with . . . the utterances of another" (Wertsch, 1991, p. 54). In essence, then, for Bakhtin, true understandings of these concepts (that is, communication) occur when speakers can effectively orient themselves with respect to one another in the broader context of conversational exchange. A key notion for Bakhtin is that "any true understanding is dialogic in nature" (Wertsch, 1991, p. 54).

The concept of voice is also key to Bakhtin's ideas pertaining to the role of language in constructing meaning. Voice applies to written as well as spoken language. It relates to point of view; "it is concerned with the broader issues of a speaking subject's perspective, conceptual horizon, intention and world view" (Wertsch, 1991, p. 51). Finally, the concept of utterance refers to Bakhtin's notion that meaning does not reside in words; rather, it resides in the ways in which words are used in particular contexts.

Bakhtin's ideas about the dialogic nature of true understanding have significant implications for instructing teachers who may work with students from vastly different sociocultural contexts. If, as Bakhtin suggests, "true understanding is dialogic in nature" (Wertsch, 1991, p. 54), teachers must pay considerable attention to their students' voices, their utterances, lives, backgrounds, and ways of thinking and reasoning, as well as to the concepts we wish to help them understand. Students' understanding is shaped to a great extent not by what we, as educators, attempt to "impart to them," but by what we understand about their thinking, by how our words are used in particular contexts, and by how we mutually (or dialogically) shape our interactions around the concepts and ideas we focus on in class.

Gee (1989) discusses the notion of cultural toolkits and argues that a primary responsibility of teachers is to acculturate students to a variety of discourse practices. This notion of acculturating students into a set of discourses is much broader than merely focusing on the form of a language. According to Gee, merely teaching students the skills of reading and writing is not enough. Rather, literacy is deeply related to social practices and cannot be separated from them. Teacher educators and classroom teachers must therefore help their students become members of various discourse communities. The teachers in my course were exposed to these and other important theoretical concepts early on so they could begin to develop practices that reflected their critical responses to these important issues.

A MODEL OF TEACHER CHANGE

The course that I designed was based on my *model of teacher change*, which emerged from my considerations of sociocultural theory and questions about how to structure teacher education to motivate teachers to become interested and skilled in working with diverse student populations, how to assist teachers in linking theory and practice, and how to facilitate the development of teacher efficacy and teachers' voices on issues of diversity.

This model emerged as I considered how teachers' evolving language practices could reflect their internal movement beyond a cognitive internalization of theory toward their becoming reflective, thoughtful, committed action agents with a personal voice to direct their further development as teachers of diverse students.

Building on Vygotsky's emphasis on the construct of mediation, I turned my attention to the powerful use of language as a cultural tool in the development of my model. I focused particularly on Wertsch's point that mediation is best thought of as a process involving the potential of cultural tools to shape action. Put another way, I focused on the value of clarifying the notion of mediation as a process involving the use of cultural tools (in this case, the strategic use of oral and especially written language) to shape action (that is, to shape or influence the development of teachers' consideration about how to become action agents or agents of change in our schools). If better understood, this notion of mediation could become a powerful tool in teacher education programs—and so my work focused on the power of using oral and written language as a pedagogical tool when facilitating the development of teachers to teach diverse student populations. To make this notion more understandable within the context of teacher education, I developed this model to explain my strategic use of language, and in particular the use of writing as a pedagogical tool for inquiry and critique, within my course as we worked to facilitate the development of teachers who truly internalized theoretical perspectives and best practices for use in their teaching of students from diverse racial, ethnic, and language groups.

Building on sociocultural theory, this model depicts the internal activity that constitutes learning as the teachers developed philosophies on diversity and commitment to action. Those developing philosophies and commitments were reflected in the texts that the teachers created for my course. Their oral and written texts yielded powerful disclosures about how the teachers were considering issues of diversity in their own minds, in their personal lives, and in their teaching. The various written texts created over time by these teachers, along with the audiotapes of class and small-group discussions that I transcribed, are a window into the teachers' developing thoughts, allowing me to monitor the thoughtful reflections of these teachers as they moved beyond mere conceptual involvement toward a commitment to action. In order to understand this process better, I drew on Bakhtin's discussion of ideological becoming, Vygotsky's discussion of internalization, Bakhtin's discussion of voice, and Leont'ev's discussion of activity when considering the stages of my model. In the sections that follow, I explain the critical role that these scholars played in the development of a theoretical framework that supported my work with the teachers in my course.

The model in Figure 4.1 reflects the processes of teachers' change and the changing discourse practices that emerge as teachers' perspectives changed. The changes included movement through four stages. We began the class by emphasizing the narrativization of teachers' experiences to motivate increased metacognitive awareness of the role of literacies in their own lives and in the lives of others. Next, the class began to emphasize reflection, introspection, and critique in the teachers' writing and discussions in order to facilitate ideological becoming. The course then focused on facilitating internalization through teacher research projects that led teachers to an increased sense of efficacy, an emergence of personal voice in their writing, and the development of plans of action. During the final stages of the course, we focused on combining theory, practice, and actual work with students from diverse racial,

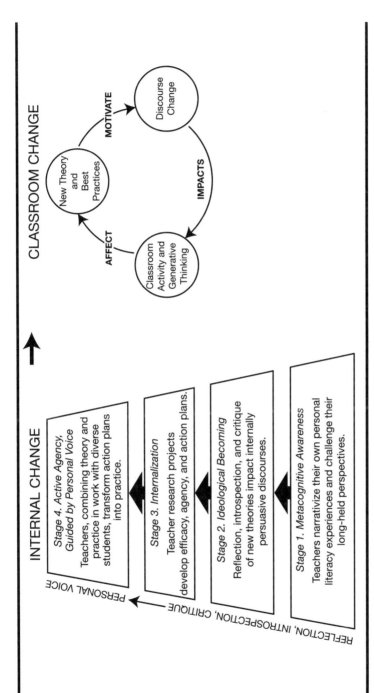

Figure 4.1. Model of teacher change: From increased metacognitive awareness to active agency and classroom change. As instruction occurs within teachers' zone of proximal development, their risk taking increases and personal voice continuously develops. The discourse also evolves over time, reflecting teachers' developing commitment.

ethnic, and language groups as a catalyst for transforming plans of action into practice. The teachers' movement through the four phases of this model was not necessarily linear. Teachers engaged more deeply in those stages that correlated with their needs and their readiness within the zone of proximal development. The use of writing as a pedagogical tool for inquiry and critique gave the teachers a medium for discovering their own thoughts and needs. It also helped the more informed others to discover how best to support the teachers. The model in Figure 4.1 shows how the course activities helped to facilitate the evolution of the teachers' language practices. This model reflects teachers' internal movement beyond mere cognitive internalization or parroting of theory as they became reflective, thoughtful, committed action agents with a personal voice to direct their generative development as effective teachers.

Using Writing as a Pedagogical Tool for Inquiry and Critique

In the early stages of my research, I made the methodological decision to use writing as a pedagogical tool in this study. I wanted to facilitate the process of pedagogical inquiry by engaging teachers in extensive writing as they struggled ideologically with issues of teaching, learning, and diversity. Inspired by the work of Dillard (1995), I approached writing from a philosophical, experimental, and pedagogical standpoint; however, unlike Dillard, my approach was grounded in the work of the sociocultural theorists Vygotsky, Bakhtin, and Leont'ev. Through writing assignments, I provided teachers with opportunities to critically examine multiple theoretical perspectives and best practices and to consider them in light of their own developing goals for teaching. I encouraged teachers to use writing to reflect on the readings and course activities; to pose thoughtful questions that emerged from the readings; and to interrogate their own pedagogy, practice, and philosophies about teaching and about their students. This writing went far beyond simple reflection on personal experiences: It was used as a pedagogical strategy that called for an analytical, introspective examination of the practices of teaching and learning as dynamic, complex, and situated in the lives of students and teachers both inside and outside the classroom. Inspired by the work of Emig (1977), Gere (1989), and Langer and Applebee (1987), I offered teachers extensive opportunities to write. In designing the course, I proposed that the actual act of inscription holds some unique properties for achieving my goal of preparing teachers for diversity; that it facilitates deep intellectual engagement and influences thinking and learning in ways not accomplished through the use of other literacies.

Emig proposes that writing represents a unique mode of learning—not merely valuable, not merely special, but unique (1977, p. 7). She distinguishes writing from verbal language processes—listening, reading, and talking—as it possesses attributes that correspond uniquely to certain powerful learning strategies. She also proposes that engagement with the act of writing involves individuals in a kind of learning that differs from other uses of literacy. The psychologists Vygotsky (1981), Luria (1981), Leont'ev (1981), and Bruner (1986, 1990) have implied that writing plays a heuristic role and that higher cognitive functions (such as analysis and synthesis) seem to develop most fully with the support of language systems that include writing. Building on the notion that learning involves the reorganization or confirmation of a cognitive scheme in light of experience, Bruner posits three major ways in which we represent and deal with actuality: (a) *enactive*, when we learn by doing; (b) *iconic*, when we learn by depiction in an image; and (c) *representational* or *symbolic*, when we learn by restatement in words. In *Thought and Language*, Vygotsky notes that writing makes a unique demand, in that the writer must engage in "deliberate structuring of the web of meaning" (1962, p. 100). This deliberate action causes the writer to think in certain structured ways that facilitate learning.

According to Emig, Luria provides one of the most powerful rationales for viewing writing as heuristic:

> Written speech is bound up with the inhibition of immediate process of immediate synpractical connections. It assumes a much slower, repeated mediating process of analysis and synthesis, which makes it possible not only to develop the required thought, but even to revert to its earlier stages, thus transforming the sequential chain of connections in a simultaneous, self-reviewing structure. Written speech thus represents a new and powerful instrument of thought. (Emig, 1977, p. 118)

In her explanation of how writing inhibits "immediate synpractical connections," Emig provides Luria's definition of synpraxis as "concrete-active" situations in which language does not exist independently but as a "fragment" of an ongoing action "outside of which it is incomprehensible" (Emig, 1977, p. 50). Put another way, "writing virtually forces a remoteness of reference on the language user" (Vygotsky, 1962). Emig further notes:

> But then he [Vygotsky] points out the relation of this slower pace to learning: this slower pace allows for—indeed, encourages—the shuttling among past, present, and future. Writing, in other words, connects the three major tenses of our experience to make meaning. And the two major modes by which these three aspects are united are the processes of analysis and synthesis: analysis,

the breaking of entries into their constituent parts; and synthesis, combining
or fusing these, often into fresh arrangements or amalgams. (1977, p. 13)

Emig focuses on the often stated but seldom substantiated claim that writing enables, or supports, thinking in unique ways. She describes how writing uniquely corresponds to powerful learning strategies, encourages others
to seriously consider the value of writing as a pedagogical tool for learning,
and describes the relationship between writing, thinking, and learning. Emig
appeals to us to consider writing as epigenetic, with the complex evolution-
ary development of thought steadily and graphically visible and available
throughout as a record of the journey, from jotting and notes to full discur-
sive formulation. My research supports Emig's arguments; as she does, I view
writing as epigenetic and use it as a steady and graphically visible tool with
which my teachers may record their journeys of discovery.

In *How Writing Shapes Thinking*, Langer and Applebee (1987) investigate writing in secondary schools to determine its use in fostering learning
and in integrating new information with previous knowledge and experience.
I use writing as a methodological approach and as a pedagogical tool in my
research in the belief that it can be used strategically to foster learning, integrate new information, and shape the thinking of developing teachers as they
consider new perspectives on working with diverse students. My research
built on that of Langer and Applebee (1987) as I studied how writing could
be used in investigations of teachers' use of written reflection, introspection,
analysis, and critiques as they went through the process of ideological change.

In addition to being informed by the arguments of Emig (1977) and
Langer and Applebee (1987) stated above, I was convinced of the utility of
writing as the focal literacy in this research because it facilitates a logical
presentation of ideas and allows us to disseminate those ideas widely. The
relative permanence of writing (as opposed to the fleeting nature of talk)
allows developing teachers to review and reflect on what they have written;
writing can thus potentially affect the development and shape of the very
ideas themselves. According to Langer and Applebee (1987), to improve the
teaching of writing is to improve the quality of thinking, because good writing and careful, rational, scientific thinking go hand in hand. They conclude
that the valuable role of writing in thinking can be conceptualized as resulting from some combination of (a) the permanence of the written word, allowing the writer to rethink and revise over an extended period; (b) the
explicitness required in writing, if meaning is to remain constant beyond
the context in which it was originally written; (c) the resources provided by
the conventional forms of discourse for organizing and thinking through new
relationships among ideas; and (d) the active nature of writing, providing a
medium for exploring implications of otherwise unexamined assumptions

(see Langer and Applebee, 1987). Like that of Langer and Applebee, my concern with the role of writing in learning is a part of my broader concern about the nature of effective instruction.

In *Roots in the Sawdust*, Gere (1989) makes a clear distinction between writing to show learning and writing to learn. She views writing to learn as a powerful means of learning. In this line of thinking, students should be given opportunities to use writing to grapple with new ideas (Britton, 1975) and to create their own webs of meaning (Vygotsky, 1962). Building on the work of Gere and her colleagues, I used writing to learn as a pedagogical strategy in my course to give attention to learning that goes beyond the assimilation of information; I wanted to emphasize the use of writing to learn as a pedagogical strategy that *"facilitates the development of better thinking and learning"* among teachers in teacher education programs (Gere, 1989, pp. 4–5; emphasis added). Drawing on the work of Emig (1977), Langer and Applebee (1987), and Gere (1989), in Figure 4.2 I summarize the new perspectives that emerged in the writing my teachers engaged in. In the sections below, I explain why I assigned these writings and how I analyzed them.

Using Narrative as a Tool for Increasing Metacognitive Awareness

Narrative is a valuable tool for helping us to understand our experiences and those of others. It is a framework through which human beings comprehend life and a vehicle for making our thoughts, actions, and feelings intelligible to others. Through narrative we can use the personal to become cognizant of others' deeply felt ideas and viewpoints and engage with the differences that would otherwise separate us. We can use Schwab's (1973, 1977, 1983) "commonplaces" as common denominators that cut across practices and experiences. These commonplaces can serve as places where learning takes place. For example, when our narratives merge with those of others or are confronted by new information, we can undergo learning experiences (Dewey, 1934, 1938) that can tacitly effect teachers' personal perspectives and practical knowledge (Connelly & Clandinin, 1985a, 1985b). As we consider issues of preparing teachers for diversity, we can use narrative to increase our metacognitive awareness of our own values, ideologies, feelings, thoughts, and behaviors. To accomplish this, we must be willing to share openly and to look to the emic views of narratives that are shared by others. Narratives shared and seriously contemplated have the potential to transform us by making the wealth that is contained in them a part of our developing understanding. In my course, I used narrativization as a tool for allowing teachers to get in touch with themselves and to reflect on literacy experiences in their own life and in the lives of others. Teachers wrote extensive autobiographies of early literacy development, which made them more metacognitively aware of issues of literacy and illiteracy and how these relate to diversity and equity in our local and global society. Gaining increased metacognitive awareness was the first step in my model that could guide teachers toward becoming effective teachers of students from diverse racial, ethnic, and language groups.

Using Reflective, Introspective, and Critical Writing as a Tool to Facilitate Ideological Becoming

Bakhtinian theory suggests that when we introduce new theories in teacher education programs, students will need to consider them in light of the long-held views about teaching that they arrive with (Bakhtin, 1981). According to Bakhtin, teachers need to struggle to assimilate two distinct categories of discourse: (a) authoritative discourse and (b) internally persuasive discourse. Because of the different properties of these two types of discourses, teachers struggle with them in different ways. Bakhtin (1981) defines authoritative discourse in the following way:

> The authoritative word is . . . so to speak, the word of the fathers. Its authority was already *acknowledged* in the past. It is a *prior* discourse. It is therefore not a question of choosing it among other possible discourses that are its equal. (pp. 342–343)

The nature of our struggles with an authoritative discourse depends on our relationship with it. We often struggle against "various kinds and degrees of authority" or against the "official line" (p. 345); such is also the case in everyday life. These struggles occur in what Bakhtin calls a "contact zone," where we "struggle against various kinds and degrees of authority" (p. 345). For the students in my teacher education course, that zone of contact included, not only our teacher education classroom, but all the spaces where we contemplated and applied the theories, perspectives, and practices we were learning about in our course. It is in these places and at those moments of struggle that we develop our expanded, ever changing ideologies. Bakhtin explains that the struggle occurs because "the authoritative word demands that we acknowledge it" (p. 342).

As teachers struggle to develop their own ideologies, they come into contact and also struggle with the discourses of everyday people. This everyday discourse is what Bakhtin calls "internally persuasive" discourse. Internally persuasive discourse has an almost opposite set of properties to those of authoritative discourse. Internally persuasive discourse is "denied all privilege, [is] backed by no authority at all, and is frequently not even acknowledged in society" (Bakhtin, 1981, p. 342). It is what each person thinks for him- or herself—it is the discourse that ultimately is persuasive to the individual. As we form our own ideas on issues, we come into contact with the everyday discourses of others, and those enter our consciousness much as authoritative discourse does. The discourses of authoritative and nonauthoritative/privileged and nonprivileged others can all influence the way we think, and they all contribute to forming what ultimately becomes internally persuasive for us. But unlike its authoritative cousin, which is well established and constant, internally persuasive discourse is subject to change and is constantly interacting with our ever evolving ideologies. Thus, a variety of discourses enter into the struggle for influence within an individual's consciousness (Bakhtin, 1981, p. 348).

At its core, all learning is social, and according to Bakhtin, the social interactions that are most effective in promoting learning are those that are filled with tension and conflict (Ball & Freedman, 2004, p. 6). Individuals struggle with the tensions that are inherent in diverse voices as they develop their own ideologies. Bakhtin (1981) argues that these struggles are needed for people to come to new understandings and in ideological becoming: "The importance of struggling with another's discourse, its influence in the history of an individual's coming to ideological consciousness, is enormous" (p. 348).

After being exposed to a wide variety of theories, perspectives, and practices in my course, and after having opportunities to write and talk about them in reflective, introspective, and critical ways, teachers went through a "process of selectively assimilating the words of others" (Bakhtin, 1981, p. 341). In my course, exposure to a wide variety of theories, perspectives, and practices that relate to issues of diversity was critical to the teachers' development: The more choices we have in words to assimilate, the greater the opportunity to learn and to change. In a Bakhtinian sense, *who* we interact with in person or in print determines *what* we stand to learn and believe in. As we are given opportunities to reflect on and critique the words and discourses of others, and to think introspectively about our own internally persuasive discourses, we create fertile ground for ideological change. It was this profound ideological change that I sought to motivate teachers to engage in.

This process of ideological becoming is so important to the development of teachers for diversity because it is through this process that teachers begin to step out on their own ideologically. Teachers thus develop the ability to stand within diverse classrooms with confidence, with a sense of ownership, and with a sense of personal efficacy when teaching culturally and linguistically diverse students.

It is this process that awakens new and independent thoughts within us, which are needed to bring a different perspective to the education of students from diverse racial, ethnic, and language groups. This is the process through which generative thinking begins to emerge on the part of teachers—generative thinking that is critical in the lives of successful teachers of diverse student populations.

Exposing teachers to various ideological points of view, approaches, directions, and values and having them write about them in reflective, introspective, and critical ways was the second step in my model, which resulted in the teachers' initiating the early stages of their own voices on issues of diversity.

Development of Plans of Action, Voice, and Efficacy

In order to become effective teachers of students from diverse racial, ethnic, and language groups, the teachers in my teacher education course needed to move beyond simply parroting information to achieve what Wertsch (1991) refers to as "internalization as appropriation." Wertsch uses the Russian words *osvoit*, meaning "to make something one's own," and *osvoenie*, "the process of making something one's own." Considering the meaning of these words helps us to understand how one can take something that belongs to others and make it one's own. From this perspective, internalization involves an interaction between thought, language, and action in which ideas and activities become, at least in part, "one's own" (Bakhtin, 1981, pp. 293–294).

As a result of the activities that teachers engaged with in my course, information that was once represented on an external level (the theories and teaching strategies of others) began to take on personal meaning for them and interacted with the teachers' prior perspectives to create newly formed perspectives. The writing of the teachers revealed that in many cases it was possible to observe aspects of internalization through teachers' changing oral and written discourse practices over time and through the reflections they shared. In the case of the teachers who participated in my course, at least two forms of evidence revealed that internalization was indeed taking place—that the theories were becoming their own: teachers' movement toward the development of a personal voice in the oral and written texts they produced and teachers' moving beyond the ideas and activities presented to them in class to generate plans of action that reflected their developing commitment.

Transforming Plans of Action into Practice Through Teacher Research

Vygotsky's ultimate concern was with human consciousness, which derives from external material reality that becomes internal (see Lee & Ball, 2005). Vygotsky argued that there is an inherent relationship between external and internal activity and that language provides the *bridge* that connects the external with the internal. Another proposed link between the external and the internal is activity. These two notions need not be viewed as conflicting or contradictory if we look at *language* as the bridge that reveals the internal activity that is taking place within the individual, whereas *activity* can be regarded as that link which serves as an outward indication that the internal activity is indeed taking place because it is being played out in the actions of the individual. In this way we can account for the importance of the transformation of theory into practice for teachers in teacher education programs. One's "actions speak louder than words"; when internalization has taken place, an individual's changing ideologies and commitments will be reflected in his or her changing discourses and actions or behaviors as triangulating evidence that internal change is taking place.

We understand that activities may be as diverse as work, play, imitation, or education, but these all have one common characteristic: They call for an integration of mental and behavioral processes directed at satisfying specific goals. Zinchenko (1962/1981) demonstrated that increased engagement with particular goal-directed actions can engender their transformation into the means for carrying out other actions. The teacher research projects in which I involved the teachers were designed to allow them to engage in a goal-oriented activity that could engender the transformation of those activities and theory into the means for developing commitment to teaching diverse students. As teachers engaged in their own teacher research projects, I looked closely at their language—their change in discourse practices over time—and their change in day-to-day practice as an indicator of their change in psychological activity.

The teachers in the course engaged in teacher research projects that were grounded in their own experiences of working with students from diverse racial, ethnic, and language groups. As an element of these projects, teachers were asked to reflect on the process of making sense of their experience and telling the story of the journey. They were asked to write a history of the steppingstones that had led them to the present—that constituted a path of inquiry that bridged the gap between teaching and researching. In order to bring the two more closely together in the minds of teachers, the teacher research they conducted was thoughtful and intentional (Burnaford, Fisher, & Hobson, 1996). Using writing as a pedagogical tool, the teachers maintained a close link between teaching, research, and reflection that was thoughtful and intentional. Nancy Atwell (1993), characterizing the central role that writing plays in her research, observed, "Writing fuels my best insight. It makes me understand things I did not know before I wrote" (p. ix). In our course, teachers thought and wrote reflectively about their classroom experiences. Their metacognitive awareness increased concerning the assignments they used in class; how to respond to diverse language patterns in their classrooms; how much controversy to introduce into the classroom; how to engage the students in higher-order thinking; how to group or not group students for learning; and whether to teach critically, in ways that would push their students to examine the established social order. In completing these projects, teachers were required to formulate a question that was of real interest to them; pay careful attention to what was going on during their work with their students from diverse racial, ethnic, and language groups; carefully describe the data they collected; and engage in a process of thoughtful discovery as they were thinking and rethinking about issues related to teaching, learning, students, and diversity.

In each case, the teacher research projects served as a catalyst for the teachers' development as reflective practitioners with a personal voice on issues related to the teaching and learning of diverse students. This development of personal voice was evidence that internal activity was indeed taking place on the part of these teachers. The teachers in today's teacher education programs must move beyond simply parroting information, to achieve internalization as appropriation; this is a process dependent on how teachers can take something that once belonged to others and make it their own (Wertsch, 1991). As the teachers engaged with their teacher research projects, they thought about incorporating the best practices and theoretical perspectives we had discussed in the course (for example, giving voice to the voiceless, teaching within the zone of proximal development, critical literacy, and issues of social justice) in ways that were meaningful for their students.

As we worked within their zones of proximal development, these teachers showed a willingness and a readiness to engage in the activities that I designed to facilitate their consideration of issues relevant to teaching students from diverse racial, ethnic, and language groups. Figure 4.1 illustrates some of the changes that took place within our classroom community. As shown in the figure, the activities were specifically designed to enable the four stages of teacher change: By generating narratives of their own literacy experiences and questioning and challenging their prior perspectives on literacy, the teachers attained *metacognitive awareness*; through reflective, introspective writing and generative thinking in response to the theories that were introduced, they segued into *ideological becoming*; and through teacher research projects they learned to create new teaching strategies based on their own interpretations of theory and map out effective plans for implementing them (*internalization*), which they subsequently used with their own students (*active agency*). All this affected their thoughts concerning the new theories and best practices that were introduced in class, which motivated changes in the teachers' discourse practices during classroom discussions and even outside the course. Moreover, it influenced the subsequent classroom activities that were the driving forces that led students to engage in progressively more complex cognitive activities. Risk taking increased in our classroom as teachers felt freer to seek out verification and validation of their ideas and beliefs from the theory, from the instructor, and from their peers. The teachers' discourses changed over time as they developed their own voice and an increased sense of efficacy and commitment.

As I analyzed the extended writings of these teachers, I noticed that there was a difference in the writing of some of the teachers that indicated the development of commitment among those teachers who actively engaged in the course, the curriculum, the assignments, and theory-enacting activities versus those who did not. Those who refused to engage in meaningful ways with the course materials and activities remained uninterested in issues of diversity. This finding did not cause me to question the accuracy of the model I developed. On the contrary, it confirmed its accuracy. As I looked for indicators of developing commitment on the part of the teachers who were experiencing ideological change and internalization, I found that those teachers who engaged meaningfully with each stage of my model experienced transformation. The presence of ideological change, internalization, and transformation was signaled as teachers engaged in the articulation of specific action plans and strategies that they intended to implement in their classrooms and their expressions of commitment—particularly since commitment is defined as "the act of taking on the charge, obligation or trust to carry out some action or policy; to make a decisive moral choice that involves a person in a definite course of action" (Webster's Third New International Dictionary, 1986). Teachers' altered pedagogical practices were another signal of that change.

DATA COLLECTION

Between 1994 and 1999, I taught this course to four groups of U.S. teachers in one teacher education program and to three groups of South African teachers in two teacher education programs; between 1995 and 2005, I conducted follow-up interviews and observations in some of the teachers' classrooms. Each course met once a week over the course of a 12- to 15-week period. The class functioned as a seminar, with the instructor and student participants making frequent presentations. The seminar encouraged the full participation of all voices in the classroom. As the course instructor, I presented theory, best practices, and shared my more than 25 years of experiences teaching diverse student populations with the class and opened my own pedagogical practices to critique. In doing so, we created a space where open discussion, inquiry, and discovery could occur. The success of this seminar course rested on the free exchange of information and uninhibited intellectual and emotional engagement by class participants. This occurred through self-critique, peer critique, and the dialogic examination of assumptions, ideas, and under-standings on the part of course participants. The students were required to conduct classroom observations, carry out interviews, document collections, and implement action-oriented research that helped them make links between the study of untapped language resources and untapped literacy resources in low-prestige dialect-speaking communities.

The data that was collected placed a heavy emphasis on the narrative voices of the teachers, which was captured in their journals—their remem-brances of the past, visions of the future, and dreams of new possibilities, which all occur most often in narrative form (Hardy, 1977). The data col-lected from these teachers included narrative essays of their own literacy autobiographies, transcripts of classroom and small-group discussions, jour-nal entries, and reflections written in response to carefully selected class readings. Students kept journal/reading logs that were ongoing, interactive journals. The weekly journal writing provided opportunities for participants to reflect on their inquiries and explorations inside and outside class that related to the course. They enabled the participants to write about ideas they found interesting, confusing, or contradictory and were expected to contain thoughtful and critical analysis of the issues discussed in class.

Data was also collected from the teachers' action research projects, conducted in classrooms serving students who were racially, ethnically, and linguistically diverse. These action research projects involved the teachers in self-reflective inquiry "in order to improve the rationality and justices of (a) their own practices, (b) their understanding of these practices, and (c) the situations in which the practices are carried out" (Kemmis, 1998, p. 42). The emancipatory action research these teachers participated in re-quired that they commit themselves not only to the development of practical skills to change classroom practice but also to the development of political consciousness that allowed them to critique the contexts of that practice (Walker, 1991, p. 167). Teachers' engagement with emancipatory action research was needed to help them understand the issues facing teacher educa-tion today and to provide a context within which they could consider how they could address the needs of marginalized students from racial, ethnic, and linguistic backgrounds that differed from their own. Emancipatory action research was in keeping with the notion of *transformative academic knowl-edge* (Banks, 1996) in that it provided a context for challenging mainstream notions of the purpose of the knowledge they were gaining. As teachers en-gaged in their emancipatory action research projects, they began to recognize instances in which the knowledge presented was not neutral and that it re-flected the power and social relationships within society. They began to think about the work they were doing as a way to help people improve society and to influence change in the socioeconomic inequalities reflected in the underresourced schools they worked in. As the teachers completed their action research projects, they developed voices of their own that helped to guide them in the generative and creative work that they were developing a commitment to doing.

Setting

I conceptualized the teacher education classroom as a setting—a contact zone (Bakhtin, 1981; Pratt, 1989)—where the narratives of teachers' experiences could be used as a tool for increasing their metacognitive awareness of the centrality of literacies in teaching and learning; where reflection, introspection, and critique could facilitate teachers' ideological becoming; where the process of internalization could take place, resulting in teachers' increased sense of efficacy, emergence of voice, and development of plans of action; and where emancipatory teacher research projects helped to plant the seeds for the eventual transforming of plans of action into practice. As teachers engaged with all of these activities, they became engaged dialogically with themselves, their peers, and the instructor and other professionals and wrote autobiographical reflective essays and narratives about their experiences and thoughts.

The classroom environment was viewed as a minisociety, where a community of learners engaged in activity, dialogic discourse, and reflection. Within this minisociety, the traditional hierarchy of teacher as the autocratic knower and learner as the unknowing, controlled subject studying to learn what the teacher knows began to dissipate as I assumed a facilitator's role and as teachers engaged with and took ownership of the ideas that were meaningful for them. Teachers' development of autonomy, mutual reciprocity of social relations, and individual empowerment became the classroom goals.

In this exploratory study, I collected the oral and written texts of more than 100 U.S. and South African teachers. The data were collected from students who participated in three teacher education programs. One secondary teacher education program was offered at a major university located in the Midwest of the United States. This teacher education program enrolled approximately 500 students each year, the majority of whom come from White working-class and middle-class homes. The students in the course were generally approximately 58% female and 42% male. About 86% of the students enrolled in the program came from nearby cities within the state, while 14% came from other states throughout the country. Approximately 74% of the students enrolled in the program came from European American backgrounds, 15% were non-White, and 11% were of unidentified heritage.

The second teacher education program was offered at a major college of teacher education located in Guatang province in South Africa. This teacher education program was designed to prepare teachers to teach in primary and secondary schools and annually enrolled approximately 200 students, the majority of whom came from White working-class and middle-class homes. More than 90% of the students enrolled in this program came from nearby cities and townships within the province. Approximately 84% of the students came from English and Afrikaans backgrounds, while about 16% were from other cultural and linguistic groups.

The third teacher education program was at a major university located in the Western Cape province of South Africa. Although the university offered a traditional teacher education program, the students enrolled in this course were participating teachers who were returning to the university to seek additional certification in a Further Diploma in Education program. This new teacher education program was designed specifically to prepare teachers to teach in multilingual and multicultural schools. It enrolled 36 students during its first term. More than 85% of the students came from nearby townships within the province and from backgrounds in which Black African languages were spoken. Fewer than 15% came from locations throughout the city that had been designated as living areas for "Coloreds" during the former system of apartheid. These students came from English- and Afrikaans-speaking backgrounds. The oral and written texts that I collected were written by these U.S. and South African teachers and reflected their developing perspectives on literacy and teaching students from diverse backgrounds.

Throughout the course, teachers integrated their own teaching and learning experiences through discussions and writings about their attempts to link theory and practice when teaching diverse student populations. Both before and after their engagement with the assigned readings and discussions, teachers wrote reflective narrative essays. These focused on teachers' own personal experiences with literacy, their developing definitions of literacy, and their developing philosophies about the use of literacy in their current and future classrooms. In their journals, the teachers reflected on the course readings and their teaching practices. Interviews and videotapes, which illustrated the teachers' implementation of theoretical principles as they worked with diverse students, were collected from a subset of these 100 teachers. Additionally, I collected audiotapes of dialogues about their actual and planned application of theory in their classrooms and, later, about the impact of the course on their day-to-day practices, their perceptions of themselves as teachers, and the roles that administrators and district supervisors should play in supporting the development of teachers.

Analysis and Findings

There were two parts to the analysis of the data: (1) a macroanalysis of the changing perspectives of the 100 U.S. and South African teachers who participated in the study concerning what it means for a person to be literate; and (2) a microanalysis of the literacy histories and reflective writings of a smaller subset of the 100 teachers to determine emerging themes that reflected changes in their developing commitment to teaching diverse student populations.

For the macroanalysis, I tallied, categorized, and summarized the teachers' initial and evolving definitions of literacy to provide an overview of the teachers' changing definitions of literacy and their changing perspectives on what it means for a person to be literate. This analysis revealed that among the U.S. and South African teachers the highest number of definitions of a literate person before their exposure to the course were limited to "the ability of individuals to communicate using reading, writing, and oral language" with few other qualifications. Only a small number of teachers conceptualized a literate person as someone who used other mediums to communicate ideas effectively. Only one U.S. teacher conceptualized the complexities of literacy to include such a feature as "critical agency in one's life."

After their exposure to the course activities and theoretical perspectives, the teachers' perspectives on literacy began to broaden considerably. Reading the U.S. teachers' literacy definitions, I noted that many of them referred to the notion of critical literacy in their definitions by the end of the course. Only a few of the South African or U.S. teachers referred to critical thinking in their initial definitions of literacy, whereas a large number of the teachers mentioned this concept in their final definitions. Several of the course participants indicated their desire to assist their students in acquiring a voice in their final definitions and they expressed the belief that critical literacy was an important tool for helping their students to acquire a voice. Two similarities between the U.S. and South African teachers' final definitions were that both groups gave responses that suggested their definitions of literacy had broadened and that their course activities had greatly expanded their conceptualizations of literacy to include a wider variety of mediums (reading, writing, oral language, computer literacies, visual literacies, and artistic literacies). One goal of the course had been to facilitate teachers' considerations about how literacies can be used in strategic ways to more effectively teach their content area materials to all students, including those from culturally and linguistically diverse backgrounds. The results of the macrolevel analysis of the data suggested that these teachers were beginning to broaden their understanding of the many different ways that an individual can be considered literate and their different ways of expressing that literacy.

The microanalysis of the literacy histories and reflective writings took place in four phases. Phase 1 consisted of a content analysis of the teachers' discourses in which I noted emerging thematic and linguistic patterns. I organized the emerging themes and linguistic patterns into broad categories to see how theory and pedagogical suggestions were "played out" in the teachers' stories of practice. This analysis provided a powerful lens through which to explain the ways these teachers conceptualized the use of literacies in their classrooms based on their own developing experience. As teachers developed, they wrote about their experiences and the theory they encountered and gave narrative form to their teaching and learning experiences— to shape them, to actively critique them, and sometimes to transform them.

Guided by the work of Stubbs (1983), Labov (1972, 1982), Gee (1991), and Bruner (1985), Phase 2 of the analysis consisted of discourse analyses that included examining the subject of independent clauses within the teachers' texts to note shifting points of view and shifting loci of agency throughout the narratives. In this analysis I noted students' uses of introspection, reflections of the "self," and developing signs of ownership by looking for uses of "I" and "me" statements in their attributions of personal voice and cultural identity to self as protagonist in their stories (Brown, 1987); uses of anecdotes and personal narrative examples; uses of affective terms; and discourse that was student centered rather than teacher or content centered.

In Phase 3 of this analysis I noted students' taking on an analytical stance in their writing as they began to challenge the existing theory that had been presented to them in prior classes. As students began to show increased agency in their writing, I noted that they used verbs and other sentence elements that indicated they were taking on personal responsibility for their students' learning and becoming more accountable for the changes that were needed in the educational system.

In Phase 4 of the analysis I noted students' theory posing in their writing and the articulation of plans of action, and I triangulated the narrative data with close examination of my field notes, the videotapes, small-group discussions that the teachers participated in, and the classroom observations of the teachers' developing practices that took place over the following few years.

Figure 4.2 provides a summary of the four phases of analysis I used. This analysis provided evidence of teachers' emerging voices, illustrated their application of theory and principles in their classrooms, and demonstrated their changing practices over time.

Three Types of Participating Teachers

Over the course of this multiyear study, my analysis of the data revealed that three types of teachers participated in the study: teachers who started the course with a commitment to issues of diversity and whose commitment seemed to become more evident throughout the term; transitioning teachers

INDICATORS OF DEVELOPMENT OF COMMITMENT, EFFICACY, AND AGENCY

Narrativization	Introspection and Reflection	Critique	Emerging Personal Voice
CHARACTERIZED BY:			
* Becoming metacognitively aware of social and cultural influences on literacy	* Taking a reflective stance * Beginning to challenge long-held personal ideas * Increased personal involvement in texts	* Taking on an analytical stance * Beginning to challenge theoretical ideas and perspectives * Synthesizing aspects of theoretical perspectives that are becoming internally persuasive * Increased personal agency and verbalizations about educational and economic inequities	* Theory posing * Envisioning new possibilities * Planning and implementing ideas consistent with developing perspective * Teacher efficacy becoming apparent
MANIFESTATIONS IN DISCOURSE			
1. Remembered stories 2. Lived experiences	1. Increased use of personal pronouns in academic writing 2. Use of anecdotes and personal narrative and examples 3. Use of affective terms 4. Student centered versus discipline centered	1. Use of verbs and sentence structures that indicate a "taking on" of personal responsibility for carrying out actions 2. Expression of personal accountability for needed change 3. Generating plans and strategies in their teacher research projects	1. Posing concrete plans and strategies to bring about what they feel needs to be happening 2. Moving beyond the theories that they have heard to pose their own ideas and theories 3. Accounts of action plans transformed to practice in their own classroom teaching

Figure 4.2. Discourse analysis as a tool for gauging the success of teacher education programs in developing teachers who are committed to teaching poor and marginalized students from diverse racial, ethnic, and linguistic backgrounds.

who initially had not given issues of diversity much consideration but who eventually displayed evidence that such a commitment was developing; and teachers who started and ended the course without developing a commitment to issues of diversity as defined in this study. While these populations are discussed further in Chapter 8, I will mention here that my analysis of the data showed that among the American teachers, approximately 26% had been committed to teaching poor and marginalized students before the course began; 44% percent were transitioning teachers who began to seriously consider teaching these students as a result of the course; and about 30% had not been committed to teaching students from diverse racial, ethnic, and language groups before the course began or after it ended. Among the South Africa teachers, approximately 30% had been committed to teaching poor and marginalized students before the course began, 48% were transitioning teachers, and 22% had not been committed to teaching students from diverse racial, ethnic, and language groups either before the course began or after it ended.

From on my observations, I concluded that—when instruction occurs within a teacher's zone of proximal development—the development of teachers' philosophies of literacy can be altered by contact with strategically selected inputs from teacher educators, theoretical readings, and interactions with colleagues when negotiated within the context of reflective writing and discussions that extend the teachers' zones of proximal development. I also concluded that in the case of teachers who started *and* ended the course without developing a commitment to issues of diversity, this course was not functioning within their zone of proximal development. One teacher who started and ended the course without developing a commitment to working with students from different racial, ethnic, and language groups shared the following reflection in his journal:

> I grew up in an upper-middle-class area and went to an upper-class high school. I admit, I did not fully realize the differences [between poor and affluent schools] until I did my pre-student teaching experience here in a working-class area. Though not an inner-city school, this school had its problems, and did hold true to many of the characterizations that our readings pointed out. However, I believe that many of the characterizations that [the articles] discussed were exaggerated and drawn out.

This preservice teacher appeared resistant to opening his mind to new ideas concerning issues of diversity. The following journal entry led me to believe that he had entered the program with limited, preconceived notions about teaching diverse students, which he was unwilling to relinquish:

> I have only incorporated two ideas [from the course] thus far that are different from what I originally thought. I plan on implementing the *I-Search* assignment as a form of building literacy, and I have enjoyed Vygotsky's (1981) work and will keep it in mind as I teach. I also enjoyed learning about the theory of constructivism. That is mainly due to the fact that I previously held ideas very similar to that of constructivism, and therefore already intended to use them, . . . only on my own terms.

This students' lack of openness to considering new ideas on diversity reflected the possibility that the concepts and activities covered in the course were not situated within his zone of proximal development. In another one of his journal entries, he noted that

> the remaining readings, especially the Bakhtin (1981) reading, failed to teach me anything. In fact, I read his chapter, attempted to summarize it, read it again, and could not remember a thing I read. Therefore, I will not bore you with quotes from his chapter, since the point of this assignment, I assume, is to show understanding of the reading, which I have not gained. I feel extremely out of touch with the material presented, and fail to see how it fits in with my concept of teaching. I realize that my concept is my own, and is probably not like that of the instructors or my classmates. I feel as though I am reading articles written by university professors who have lost touch with the common folk.

The comments made by this and several other students in the program helped me to understand how preservice teachers can graduate from teacher education programs lacking the knowledge needed to become excellent teachers of diverse students. Students' unwillingness to reread articles to locate their main points or to grapple with difficult issues through writing signaled a resistance that would be difficult to penetrate. For an activity to play itself out within an individuals' zone of proximal development, the person must first be willing to become socially and intellectually engaged in ways that meaning can be drawn from the activity. According to Tharp and Gallimore (1988):

> Teaching occurs only when assisted performance is provided to the learner in the ZPD. To achieve this ideal requires, of those who would be teachers, a transformation of the mind. This transformation consists in the development of new, higher-order cognitive processes, new values, and new motives. (p. 249)

A transformation of the individual is unlikely in situations where the individual refuses to engage socially or cognitively in the activity that is occurring. Darling-Hammond (1992) notes that the consequences of this transformation *not* taking place is that many underprepared teachers will leave their teacher education programs without the knowledge needed to guide the development of their students, and these teachers will be less likely to see it as their responsibility to identify and meet the needs of their students. She further comments that all too often, these teachers blame their students when the former's teaching is not successful. I found this to be true in the case of several participants in each of my courses. I never lost sight of the hope, however, that by requiring every course participant to engage with important issues that centered on diversity, the possibility always existed that, having engaged with these issues during the course, they could always reflect back on these issues at a later date and perhaps take a positive and enlightened stance on issues of diversity in the future. As Cazden (1988) remarks:

> It is important not to have a mechanical conception of the process of internalization whereby overt social interaction (speaking and listening) becomes transformed into covert mental processes (thinking) . . . [that] the learners somehow figure out for themselves. . . . In teaching, therefore, we should not assume a one-to-one relationship between the components of mature performance and the ingredients of the most effective instruction. As with children's language development, the models provided are samples to learn from, not examples to learn. The heart of human cognition is the ability to discover new ideas, to "go beyond the information given," in Bruner's apt phrase. . . . Englestrom's general point is important: scaffolds as an instructional model cannot account for the mental leap to a new idea. (pp. 107–108)

Cazden's points are well taken, that learners must somehow figure things out for themselves. Discovering new ideas and going beyond the information that is given to them assumes some effort on the part of the learner. Intellectual transformation and internalization are not processes that can be mechanically imposed on students. The theory, best practices, and activities provided in my course were designed to serve as scaffolds that would support students in their learning—learning that would help them make the *mental leap* needed to become effective teachers of diverse student populations.

I have shared the voice of one nontransitioning student because his experience was typical of many of the teachers who came into the course without a commitment to diversity and left the course without making any apparent growth toward an openness to working with diverse students. Students' decisions to limit their engagement with the ideas, theory, and practices that are presented to them in the course limits their ability to make the mental leap to new ideas, attitudes, and skills that they would need to work effectively with students from culturally and linguistically diverse populations. Just as sociocultural theory helps to explain the success of my work with many teachers, it also helps to explain my lack of success with the nontransitioning teachers. Sociocultural theory helps us to understand that the different backgrounds, dispositions, attitudes, and cognitive abilities that teachers bring to the learning environment will influence the success of teacher education programs in reaching their expressed goals of preparing teachers to work with students from different racial, ethnic, and language groups.

The stories that follow in Chapters 5 to 8 focus on the process of teacher change as revealed through the developing discourse practices of transitioning teachers and their subsequent behavior. The eight individuals discussed in these chapters were selected as the focus teachers for this book because they were a representative sample of the many teachers I observed in cases when my instructional practices fell clearly within their zones of proximal development. Consequently, my instructional practices combined with the other experiences in these teachers' lives to affect their internalization processes most significantly.

Following are brief descriptions of the eight focal teachers, whose case studies indicated that we were functioning within their zones of proximal development during and following the course.

Irene

Irene was one of the South African teachers who enrolled in my teacher education course. She was in her mid-20s and came from a middle-class background. Irene attended a teacher education program that was offered at a major university located in Western Cape province. Although the university offered a traditional teacher education program, Irene was enrolled in a course for current teachers who were seeking further certification in a Further Diploma in Education program. This teacher education program was designed to prepare teachers to teach in multilingual and multicultural schools. When I first met Irene she was an early-career teacher who lived and taught in an area of the city that had been designated as a living area for "Coloreds" during the former system of apartheid.

Jim

When I first met Jim, he was a 23-year-old beginning teacher who came from a European American family in one of the western U.S. states. In his youth, Jim liked to read stories about boys much like himself. He grew up in a farmhouse, without much money. Jim attended a secondary teacher education program at the flagship university in a midwestern state. He taught math classes in an urban school environment while working on certification and a masters of arts degree in education.

Nomha

Nomha was a South African female teacher who enrolled in my teacher education course while I was teaching at a major university located in Western Cape province in South Africa. Nomha came from a Black-African-language-speaking background and began her schooling at a lower primary school in one of the Black townships. In her late 20s/early 30s when we met, Nomha had been teaching in a township school for a few years with class sizes of 60 to 65 students. At the beginning of the course she was very shy and soft-spoken, but I sensed that she was eager to learn about theory and new pedagogical strategies. She had received her teaching credential from a teachers' college that had been established to train Black teachers to teach Black students. She had returned to the Further Diploma in Education program offered at the university in order to receive further training.

Mosola

Mosola was a teacher who came from a Black South African family in the southern Cape. His grandmother had been a principal at one of the local schools and a dedicated teacher who usually held weekend classes at her home; she was strict and not only engaged her students in recitations, but also pushed them to go to the library and to explain to others what their books were about. Mosola recalled that his grandmother liked sitting with her students and telling them stories. While this early training sometimes frustrated Mosola, it helped him to prepare for further schooling and opportunities in his education when he would be selected to teach the class and be the teachers' special helper. These experiences helped him to gain confidence in himself. When I returned to South Africa in 2000, Mosola was still teaching high school classes in a senior secondary school, but he had recently been promoted to head of his department.

Mieko

Mieko was a 23-year-old female of Asian American descent who attended a teacher education program that was offered at a major university located in the midwestern region of the United States. This program enrolled each year approximately 500 students, the majority of whom came from White working-class and middle-class homes. Although Mieko was a preservice teacher from a middle-class background, she became engaged with the thought of teaching poor, marginalized, and underachieving students in a U.S. inner-city community.

Monica

Monica was a middle-class, African American student in her early 20s who was attending a preservice teacher education program offered at a major university located in the midwestern region of the United States that served mostly White middle-class students. While Monica was attending a preservice teacher education program, she had done some substituting and course observations in mostly middle-class schools like the one she herself had attended.

Niko

Niko was an Asian American teacher from a middle-class community in the midwestern United States. Niko grew up attending well-resourced schools and was always taught in a positive, empathetic and understanding atmosphere. She always felt that her teachers sincerely wanted to make her learning environment an enjoyable and productive place. Niko's interest was piqued by the realization that all students did not receive this type of education, and she was developing a deep interest in working with some of our society's most needy populations. The writings that Niko produced in my class revealed her openness to considering new ideas.

Gafumbe

Gafumbe was one of the more mature, experienced teachers in our Further Diploma in Education program. With many years of experience teaching in a Black township school, Gafumbe was returning to the university course for further study. He noted that he had much to learn and felt that he could learn new things from every situation in which he found himself. He participated in a teacher education program that was offered at a major university located in Western Cape province in South Africa. Although the university offered a traditional teacher education program, the students enrolled in this course were current teachers who were seeking additional certification. Gafumbe came from a poor, Black African-language-speaking background.

In the chapters that follow, I present the literacy histories and reflective writing of these eight focus teachers. As I trace these teachers' discourse development I provide evidence of their developing commitment through their reflections on their life experiences and on the course readings, discussions, and activities. Building on Vygotsky's notion of the developmental or genetic method, these data are shared with the assumption that teachers' self-reports have value and that they can be used to help capture the cognitive and psychological processes that teachers experience.

ROLE OF THE RESEARCHER

While I have tried as much as possible to let my informants speak for themselves, this account is, of course, informed by my own experiences as a student, teacher, teacher educator, and researcher. As an African American female, I have lived and worked for most of my professional life in communities not unlike the ones I am preparing teachers to work in. Much of what I heard from the participants during my years of data collection was influenced by my own experiences over the years. I have worked hard at being as unbiased as possible in my accounts of these teachers' development, juggling my desire to allow the voices of the teachers to be heard with the challenge of presenting only what I wanted to hear. While I do not claim to be completely "objective" in my presentation of the portraits that follow, I can say that they were informed by an ongoing monitoring of my own biases and responses. My fondest hope is that I have fulfilled my promise to share the voices of the teachers with whom I worked with the larger educational community and that, in hearing these voices, others will better understand how to facilitate the development of more teachers to work effectively with students from different racial, ethnic, and linguistic groups and that this work might be viewed as an invitation for others to join in the global dialogue and cross-national communications about how teacher education programs can best meet the challenges posed by the growing diversity in our student populations.

An Awakening to New Light: Increasing Metacognitive Awareness Through Narrative

Sharing the Voices of Mieko, Gafumbe, and Mosola

AN AWAKENING TO NEW LIGHT

The birth of a baby elephant in the wild is a grand and social occasion. There is a sense of excitement in the air. Within minutes after birth, the mother attempts to help the newborn rise to its feet. This is a matter of survival since the newborn must be able to stand on its own to gain sustenance. Without this, the calf is sure to perish.

Like many other infants in the animal kingdom, a baby elephant begins life with poor vision. But with proper stimulation, time, nurture, and maturation, the calf's vision improves rapidly. As the first morning dawns, the baby elephant's vision is already improving. And as the sun filters through the trees, the sky becomes brighter, new light floods in, and things become clearer. These first moments in the life of the calf entail much change. Images that once seemed far off and veiled in a cloudy blur, become clear and focused.

In this way, the developing baby elephant is similar to the developing preservice teacher. Both begin a new situation with limited vision . . . but with proper stimulation their minds are opened to new light. The birth of an elephant calf in the wild is an exciting event for the entire herd. The calf becomes the center of attention, receiving care and protection from all members of the herd. The birth of a new teacher is likewise a celebrated event. Through a social system called a teacher education program, novice teachers gain the experiences and expertise they need to sustain and enrich their professional lives and the lives of their students. The way these teachers come to see the world is highly dependent on the stimulation they receive and the thoughts they ponder, for this can influence their outlook and their perspectives as they begin to focus on issues outside their realms of prior awareness. Developing teachers who receive proper stimulation within the contexts of teacher education programs can become metacognitively aware of the critical role that literacies play in their lives and in the lives of others, and they can eventually come to see the urgent need for excellent teachers to become committed to teaching students from diverse cultural and linguistic backgrounds.

I N THE TEACHER EDUCATION course I taught, I used teachers' own narratives to open their vision to new light. I drew on images and experiences that once seemed blurred and far off to help teachers see current issues in a clearer and more focused way—to increase their metacognitive awareness. The term *metacognitive awareness* refers to the development of a *conscious* awareness of one's own knowledge and the *conscious* ability to reflect on, understand, control, and manipulate one's own cognitive processes. Narrative is a valuable tool for developing metacognitive awareness—for helping us to develop a conscious understanding of our own experiences and a conscious understanding of the experiences of others. It is a framework through which human beings comprehend life and a vehicle for making our thoughts, actions, and feelings intelligible to others. Through narrative we can use the personal to become aware of deeply felt ideas and perspectives and engage with the differences that would otherwise separate us.

USING NARRATIVE AS A TOOL TO INCREASE METACOGNITIVE AWARENESS

As we consider issues of preparing teachers for diversity, we can use narrative to increase our metacognitive awareness of our own values, ideologies, feelings, thoughts, and behaviors. To accomplish this, we must be willing to look introspectively and truthfully and to share openly what we find. Then we must be willing to look to the emic views of narratives that are shared by others. Narratives shared and seriously contemplated have the potential to transform us by making the wealth that is contained in them a part of our developing understanding. Gaining increased metacognitive awareness was the first step in my model of teacher change—a model that I used to guide teachers toward becoming effective teachers of students from diverse racial, ethnic, and language groups.

NARRATIVES OF TEACHERS' EXPERIENCES

The teachers began the course by writing narrative autobiographies of their own literacy experiences. This exercise was designed to increase metacognitive awareness of their journey toward becoming literate individuals and of the critical role that literacy had played in their own lives. We then engaged with biographical readings about literacy in the lives of others: *Lives on the Boundary*, excerpts from *The Long Walk Home*, *Hunger of Memory*, *Cry the Beloved Country*, *Amish Literacies*, and *The Freedom Writers Diary*. In addition, we spent a great deal of time considering issues of discourse because, as Giroux

(1988) points out, both prospective and in-service teachers need to recognize discourse as a form of cultural production, one that organizes and legitimates specific ways of naming, organizing, and experiencing social reality.

The students also read Jean Anyon's (1981) "Social Class and School Knowledge," in which she discusses the differences in school structures, school philosophies, and practices of schooling based on the four different school contexts she studied. She investigated four types of schools serving different populations. The first was a working-class school in which the dominant themes include issues of active and passive resistance to teachers' attempts to impose the curriculum. The second was a middle-class school—one in which the dominant themes focused on possibility and a belief that if one worked hard in school, one could go far in society. The third type was the affluent professional school where extreme individualism, personal development, and creativity were stressed. The fourth was the executive elite school in which the dominant themes included excellence, intense competition, and taking responsibility for oneself. Anyon found that not only did appearances inside and outside the schools differ based on location and the social class of the predominant population served, but also there were differences in curriculum, teacher quality, and the ways in which the school staff perceived the capabilities of students. After reading this article, many U.S. and South African students began to question whether we lived in a meritocracy and whether all students actually stood a fair chance of succeeding. Some students began to see the need for advocacy to ensure equal opportunity and access for all students.

LITERACY, DISCOURSE, AND POWER

In order to encourage teachers to think broadly about the role of literacy in the lives of others, we read James Gee's (1989) "What Is Literacy?" Gee suggests that teachers should think of discourse as an "identity kit" that comes complete with appropriate costume and instructions on how to act and talk so one may take on a particular role that others will recognize. Further, he presents five important points about discourse that teachers should be aware of: Discourses are inherently ideological and involve a set of values and viewpoints; discourses are resistant to internal criticism and self-scrutiny; discourse-defined positions from which we speak and behave are defined as standpoints taken up by the discourse in its relation to other, opposing discourses; any discourse puts forward certain concepts, viewpoints, and values at the expense of others, and, in so doing, marginalizes viewpoints and values central to other discourses; and discourses are intimately related to the distribution of social power and hierarchical structure in society.

After engaging with this reading, developing teachers were more aware of the reality that control over certain discourses can lead to the acquisition of social goods and that these discourses empower those who have the least conflict with dominant discourses. This realization generally made a strong impression on the developing teachers in my course. Their subsequent reading of Lisa Delpit's (1992) "Acquisition of Literacy Discourse: Bowing Before the Master?" allowed them to consider some different perspectives on those whose primary discourse is the privileged one in society and on the acquisition of discourses of power by students of color, and it provided insights on the important role they could play as their students acquired and learned secondary discourses.

HIDDEN LITERACIES

The article "Hiding Out in Secondary Classrooms" (Brozo, 1990) was introduced to teachers in our course to help them understand the coping strategies of poor readers in their classrooms. Brozo argues that teachers who only recognize effective instruction as seen from their own viewpoint fail to appreciate the needs of unsuccessful students and may inadvertently reinforce the students' failure. The teachers in my course were appreciative of Brozo's recommendations for improving teacher interactions with underachieving students.

After reflecting on the issues raised in these readings, the teachers began to broaden their definitions of what it meant for a person to be literate and began to comprehend the dire consequences of illiteracy in a global society. Subsequent to these readings, the goal of helping students become literate, critical thinkers across content areas began to emerge as a central concern for many of the teachers in my course.

The teachers' narratives, literacy histories, and reflective journal entries illustrate the changes the teachers displayed as they gained increased metacognitive awareness. As their metacognitive awareness increased, the way was opened for them to experience ideological becoming and the internalization of theory and best practices, and then to move beyond internalization to positions of efficacy, agency, and personal commitment to teaching students from diverse racial, ethnic, and language groups. The development of personal voice that emerged in the teachers' writing and class discussions was evidence that internal activity—internal change—was indeed taking place.

The course emphasized the centrality of literacies in teaching and learning. Diverse teacher populations brought a wide range of experiences and internally persuasive discourses to the course, which had an affect on their individual processes of change. Through their diverse perspectives, they recognized the existence of a rich and complex "contact zone" inside our classroom, which would yield numerous opportunities for them to decide what would become internally persuasive for them and to develop their own ideologies as related to issues of diversity. In what follows, I share excerpts from the teachers' writing.

INCREASING METACOGNITIVE AWARENESS

In this section, I focus on the writing of three teachers, Mieko, Gafumbe, and Mosola, to illustrate how they used autobiography to raise their metacognitive awareness. The excerpts that follow demonstrate how writing served as a catalyst for generative thinking on the part of these teachers and helped move them toward the eventual emergence of increased efficacy and personal voice as well.

Mieko, a 26-year-old Asian American teacher, shared the following about her own early literacy experiences in the initial autobiography she wrote:

> My mother might place the blame on my childhood love affair with the TV, or perhaps on my then intolerance of carrots. I happen to know, however, that the sole culprits were those books. If it had not been for all those books I devoured in my elementary school years, I might very well have avoided my current legally-blind-if-not-for-eyeglasses status. Instead, I am doomed to wear these Coke-bottle glasses for eternity. Was it worth it?
>
> I started reading as a hobby when I was in the third grade (coincidentally, the year I would be introduced to eyeglasses). I remember . . . I would immerse myself . . . as I'd read about the adventures of . . . wonderful characters, . . . and then, for some reason I have yet to fathom, along with my junior and high school years came the doldrums of my literacy career. The only books I opened were of the "Cliff Notes" variety, and the occasional required article or textbook. Perhaps it was considered uncool to read; of this I have no recollections. This period was to extend into my university years and to end only upon my graduation.
>
> As suddenly as my illiterate spell fell upon me, it disappeared. In the years that I lived in New York as a banker and later as a graduate student, I read everything I could lay my hands on. . . . I lost myself in the author's vivid storytelling.

As Mieko experienced increased metacognitive awareness about her own literacy experiences, she began to link old knowledge with newly introduced concepts and shared some of her emerging insights.

After Mieko recounted her early memories related to literacy and as her perspectives on literacy expanded, she could think more clearly about some of the decisions she made later in life, this clarity increasing as she engaged in her writing. In her journaling she later recalls: "I have never liked to write. And happily, not much writing has been required of me in the classes of my major: math and chemistry." While Mieko confessed that she "dreaded writing the weekly journals required for our class," she admitted:

> As I struggled with [the weekly journals], I could not help but appreciate their merit. Writing about an article seems to be the best way to understand it. Had it not been for the requisite journal, I would not have pondered the author's intended purpose in reading his work, or extended his ideas, and searched for applications to my own classroom. Writing a journal about the articles I had read forced me to think about the material; rather than simply absorb it, perhaps to be forgotten later.

One of my primary goals in requiring the teachers to write about their own literacy experiences was to allow them opportunities to engage in the two major modes by which we connect the past, present, and future—the processes of analysis and synthesis (Emig, 1977, p. 13). Through this autobiographical writing, Mieko engaged in analysis, breaking down her own literacy experiences into some of its constituent parts. She engaged in synthesis in her writing as well, fusing entries in fresh and generative ways as she questioned:

> But would journal writing elicit the same effect from my 10th graders in a geometry class? In planning to incorporate journal writing into my class routine next school year, I am betting that it will, at the very least, encourage my students to invest a little thought into the topic being discussed. All too often, I find that my students forget or incorrectly apply recently "learned" material. Writing a journal (and writing in general) about the topics discussed in class will hopefully help them organize, understand, and etch the material in their minds, as it has [helped] me.

For Mieko, autobiographical and reflective writing raised her metacognitive awareness as it facilitated generative thinking about her future teaching. She began by recounting her early literacy experiences in a light, entertaining manner, but as she became more metacognitively in tune with her own literacy experiences, she came to realize that although she enjoyed reading, she had never liked to write. It was through her engagement with extended writing in the class that she came to recognize that writing had played a major role in increasing her understanding of the course readings. It was also through her engagement with extended writing that she began to contemplate the use of writing as a pedagogy tool with her 10th-grade geometry students. In her final reflection, Mieko drew some conclusions about relationships between outdated instructional practices, her reading experiences in this class, and her continuing search for ways to encourage thinking on the part of students in her classroom:

> Andrea Fishman's *Amish Literacy* supports my developing voice on my rejection of direct instruction. I agree with her assertion that the mode of instruction presently prevalent in America's high schools is outdated. Direct instruction works for Amish students, and it worked for mainstream society half a century ago. But it is inappropriate for today's schools. Students in my classroom do not know how to think, and this "lack of thinking" is fostered in direct instructional classrooms. I have a good feeling for what does not work and in what direction I must proceed to encourage my students to think, but I'm not sure how I will apply this. I've tried to include a lot of group work in my class, but I have a feeling there's a lot more structure I must supply in their group problem sessions. I'm just not sure how.

Mieko is now able to clearly articulate her rejection of an overdependence on direct instruction, stating that the manner of instruction is inappropriate and outdated for today's schools because the students in her classroom are not being encouraged to think. As a result of her metacognitive awareness of the impact of this teaching approach on her students, she is able to say with confidence, "I have a good feeling for what does not work and in what direction I must proceed to encourage my students to think." She also plans to include lots of group work and more structure during problem-solving sessions.

Gafumbe, a South African teacher, noted that "until most recently, the term *literacy* meant the ability to read and write. And that was all! But as time has gone by in this course, I have had quite a number of new questions around this term—like the whats and the whys." Using autobiographical writing to raise his metacognitive awareness about his own literacy development, Gafumbe recalled:

What we were taught at school—from the beginning—was what was known by or to the teacher—or possibly other people—but it was not related to my own experiences.

This pattern was followed when we started learning English and Afrikaans, whose phonetics were totally different from the Xhosa version. For instance, the sound *f* in English is pronounced in *phone*, in Afrikaans it is pronounced in *vat*, and in Xhosa in *futha*. This example and a lot of others presented us with problems in spelling or dictation. The concept of *f* (as in my example) was never introduced in context. Yet failure to reproduce correctly was still a recipe for punishment.

When sentences and paragraphs were introduced, the same patterns followed—adding misery to confusion. The shortest route that we followed was to memorize everything that was taught and then reproduce what the teacher knew. That was what was considered literacy—being able to read and write what the teacher knew. These are the whats and the whys that always come into my mind when I have to think of literacy.

My sources for gaining or acquiring literacy in the broadest sense were confined to the four walls of my school, and the sole bringer of knowledge was the teacher. Knowledge was, therefore, limited and confined to those who had the rare privilege of getting beyond the primary school. It was only at about Standard 6 or 8 that sharing of knowledge really had an influence on my learning. Then we had to write reports and essays, read library books, debate, and consult, in order to complete our assignment. It was then that we began to understand that literacy is sometimes much bigger than mere reading and writing—but it was understanding what is around us.

After reflecting on his own process of becoming literate, Gafumbe easily shifted into reflections on why he chose to become a teacher. While he was engaged in the act of writing, it seemed that his metacognitive awareness was increasing as he began to elaborate (without any prompting) on literacy in the lives of others and the hunger for educational literacy among Black South Africans:

I have quite a number of reasons why I decided to become a teacher. Initially there existed a need from my parents to have something that was going to empower me in life. Money—to be honest—was one of the reasons why I was sent to a teacher-training school before I even matriculated. As years went by, I realized that there was a great need, a great hunger, for Black South Africans to be educated. During those years (1970s), it was a privilege for those who could afford to be educated. The high drop-out rates and the lack of employment opportunities in the job market instilled a sense of guilt within me. The need to be an educator was further strengthened as I realized the marginalization of those who did not have the opportunity of going through the schooling system.

Along with Gafumbe's increased metacognitive awareness came his articulate reflective responses to our course readings by Au (1994) and McElroy-Johnson (1993). Building from his own experiences of having teachers who neglected to relate learning to students' lives, Gafumbe became an advocate for building on students' background knowledge and encouraging the development of students' voices in order to teach more effectively:

> I agree with our reading by Au because I believe that we should represent diverse perspectives in our teaching. People in general have strengths and weakness on which they can build to empower themselves. . . . The same applies to the learning of a second language. To devalue the voice and the background experiences of our learners is like venturing unarmed into a bleak future for our students as learners and for us as teachers.
>
> McElroy-Johnson (1993), in "Teaching and Practice: Giving Voice to the Voiceless," distinguishes between two types of voices: the audible and the inaudible voices, which are found within individuals. The audible voice is clear and distinct, progressive and inquiring. This is found in situations where effective learning really takes place. On the other hand, there is the inaudible or the silent voice, which is not coming out to challenge, to experiment, and to visualize situations as they present themselves to the educators and the learners. The notion that "everybody has a different voice, just as every person has a different genetic inheritance" was emphasized in your teaching and this made a great influence on my understanding of literacy. The value that is given to a person's background and inputs has really influenced heavily on my general view of the learning act.

For Gafumbe, reflective and autobiographical writing served to raise his metacognitive awareness about literacy in his life and in the lives of his students. This increased metacognitive awareness led to generative thoughts concerning better ways to teach. The following excerpt from his writing illustrates this process:

It is now my conviction that voices should not be suppressed, ig-
nored, or undermined. Instead, it is essential that voices should be
encouraged, developed so that they could be heard at school, in the
community, the country, and the whole world. It is essential, therefore, that teachers ought to be democratic enough so as to allow the
learners . . . to be bold to venture into the world—best armed with
tools that they can utilize in interpreting what is going on around
them.

When I started this class I thought in the simplest terms about
what it means to say that a person is literate—that the person is able
to read and to write. I am now much more aware that literacy also
means to be able to utilize what you have in your background, to add
to it what you are engaged in so that in the future it can be a useful
tool for venturing into new situations that one finds oneself [in].

It is becoming clear to me that without knowledge there can be
no power, and vice versa. In the past, education planners in South
Africa have made the mistakes of imposing the types of learning that
they deemed to be appropriate for people. However, prior knowledge
instills confidence in the learning act . . . and the representation of
diverse views transform, empower, and redefine students' literacy
through the teaching and learning act. I believe that if we can build
from the home experience of our students, then they can move from
there to the community, to the country, and to the universe.

For Gafumbe, developing an increased metacognitive awareness of the
role and function of literacy in his life and in the lives of others was only the
first step in his developmental journey. In his final journal entry, he displayed
a strong sense of efficacy and voice:

I have—during the course of your stay at [this college]—come to
realize the importance of literacy to all people. Not only to become
literate in one's own language—but literacy in general. Literacy in
simple terms has previously meant only reading and writing to me.
With the constant collaboration with you on this issue (not just a
simple dumping of your information on me) I have found out that
there is more to literacy than just form and structure of the written
and spoken word. Literacy—now I am aware—is a very useful tool
that one has to be armed with so that one may grow, and it has
social, political, and economic implications.

As a result of this class, I have begun to ask, "How does one
then grow?" I am concluding that there are many factors that are at
play in the growth of an individual. One of which is the fact that no

person is an island. This class is giving new meaning to the phrase "Umntu Ngumntu Ngabantu" (a person is a person through associating with other people). This African concept is rich among the African people. It now has meaning also when we are involved in the learning act. Previously, in the learning act, South African learners have been viewed as "blank slates" on which information has had to be written on by the educators—the people who "know all." Your presence here has helped me question this, and articulate my opposition to this perspective. I am now feeling confident, armed and ready to negotiate meaning, to value my learners, to give voice to the voiceless, and to develop the low literacy levels of the pupils that I come in contact with.

Mosola's writing also vividly illustrates how autobiographical and reflective writing can raise metacognitive awareness. In his writings, he reflected on his early literacy experiences:

In primary school I was very shy. . . . I was a very quiet student especially when I was doing my Standard 5. I was very afraid to lift my hand up or talk because I knew if I made a mistake our teacher never hesitated to take a switch and beat us. So I felt the best thing to do was to be quiet. I never wanted to be wrong even if I was given an assignment or homework, especially math; as a result I used to wake up very early in the morning and go to school only to copy the exercise from one girl who knew math and who was always right in class. I therefore felt that I must take it that I didn't know math very well myself.

But all that changed when I was in Standard 6. I do not know what our math, English, and General Science teacher saw in me and my friend who was a girl, but he used to take us to the laboratory and do an experiment which in turn we would go and do it ourselves in the classroom for other students. In other words, we ended up teaching it to the classroom. Out of that, I realized my potential and the ability I had. As a result, when I got to the high school I was one of those who mastered math and from then I got another teacher who cared very much for his students and still made me to love math. As a result I never wanted to disappoint him by failing when I knew he knows I know his subject.

The teacher who gave me positive thinking in my math and science thinking happens to be here with me in this Further Diploma in Education class and unfortunately he does not know how much he contributed to my learning.

Mosola wrote in an introspective manner as he recalled being a shy learner who opened up to new light as a result of the encouragement of his Standard 6 teacher. He noted that his teacher did not even realize the influence he had had on Mosola's development. Mosola's writing in my class provided him an opportunity to articulate his increased awareness of and appreciation for the strong influence his former teachers had had on him. In his further writing he discussed his teaching goals and his desire to influence his students as literate individuals:

> I want to make my students realize their goals in life and bring about self-realization and confidence. I want to enable my students to be able to think for themselves, to draw knowledge out of my students and plough it back to build a nation.

In a way reminiscent of Atwell's (1993) experience, Mosola's writing gave him an opportunity to articulate some critically important realizations—that he became a teacher in order to assist in the nation-building process and that he has found a sense of belonging in the teaching fraternity. He does not discount the challenges and difficulties of this job, but he has come to realize that it is a calling that requires a commitment to his profession and, most important, to his students. As Mosola continued to write reflectively in response to our course readings, he began to think in generative ways about Vygotsky, scaffolding, and curricular reform:

> This man, Vygotsky, has had quite an impression on me and on my teaching. The theory helps me to prompt and understand my students; in that I will be able to look at what is happening between the known and unknown so that I can be able to give support where necessary. I realized this during the process of my teacher research project and after finishing that research.
>
> Unlike some of the teachers I had in my early years of learning, I will be patient with my students; I will help my students to do for themselves and only mediate where necessary. It is because of this man, Vygotsky, that I have begun to scaffold assignments for my students. My definition of literacy has expanded as a result of this course. Literacy does not only include reading and writing but also taking into consideration the cultural background of students. It is to be able to express yourself openly without fear. Literacy also involves the ability to voice your thoughts orally. Literacy involves ability to interpret what your surroundings are like. Literacy is knowing and realizing the imbalances of society and using literacy to reverse the injustices that must be made right.

The education system is supposed to teach the society (students) values of self-reliance, self-respect, and economic empowerment. The curriculum therefore should be geared towards that. It should be a curriculum which is radically changed to suit the needs of the broader society; a curriculum which deploys students in all levels of the learning process.

For Mieko, Gafumbe, and Mosola, autobiographical and reflective writing resulted in increased metacognitive awareness, which led to the generation of new ideas on issues related to their day-to-day teaching and learning and literacy. After many classroom hours were spent in reflective, autobiographical writing and discussions, mental bridges were formed that linked their own experiences with those of their students and promoted critical awareness of how they would use this new information to improve the literacy lives of their students. Using writing as a pedagogical tool, Mosola, Gafumbe, and Mieko all became clearer about their teaching goals and the principles that would guide them in "using literacy to reverse the injustices that must be made right," as Mosola put it so well.

The Process of Coming into Our Own: Creating Spaces for Reflection, Introspection, and Critique

Sharing the Voices of Monica and Niko

COMING INTO OUR OWN

Baby otters mature very slowly. It takes 5 to 7 weeks before their eyes are even open. But by 3 months of age, they have finally shed their baby fur for the thick, waterproof coats they'll need in order to begin swimming lessons. Otters are well suited for life in the water. With their long bodies and webbed feet, mature otters become excellent swimmers. They paddle with their hind legs, move their powerful tails, turn somersaults in water, and are quite the acrobats. Strangely enough, otters are not born knowing how to swim. Mother otters must teach their pups how to survive in the water. At first, she plays water games with them. When the young pups are ready, she pushes them into the water and, as they try to swim, mother otter stands ready to rescue her floundering pups. She coaxes and encourages them through every step. Through repetition and trial and error, they learn to swim and build bridges in their minds that link their prior experiences with the new information that is presented to them.

Young otters will initially chase anything that moves, but they soon learn to become skillful underwater hunters. While all otters are very playful animals, the mother otter has a serious side, too. She's a skilled hunter and a faithful parent. She has the baby otter slide repeatedly down the muddy riverbank to learn how to travel in snow. She must get the pups to contemplate the challenges in their world. This is accomplished by regularly exposing them to new experiences.

But the mother otter does not accomplish this alone. Both mother and father share in raising the young. The female is watchful as the male greets his offspring and takes over as teacher. Encouraged by the examples of these role models, coaxed from in front as well as from behind, the youngster finally takes to the water. At first, its swimming is more dog paddle than ballet. His learning is slow and steady. But little by little, the young otter, overwhelmed by curiosity, forgets for a few moments that he has never dived or held his breath in the water. And by the time he does remember, it's too late for panic; he already knows how. There's nothing to do but go back for a bit of practice.

Baby otters are much like developing teachers in that, through exposure to new experiences, through trial and error, and through repetitive
activities, they learn to build bridges in their minds that link their prior perspectives and experiences with the new information that is presented to
them. Through these methods, they contemplate the possibilities and challenges of the work before them, and they critically examine their worldviews
and ideologies concerning that world. As developing teachers are exposed
to new perspectives and write reflectively about them, they become aware
of the consequences of literacy and the discrepancies between their long-
held views about teaching, learning, and diversity and the new ideas they
encounter. In this way, they begin to swim, even if it means going against
the tide, or standing on their own two feet.

ONCE TEACHER EDUCATION programs have accomplished the goal
of helping teachers become metacognitively aware of the role that literacy
has played in their lives and in the lives of their students, then bridges can begin
to form in their minds that link their prior perspectives with the new information
that is presented to them in class. The need still remains, however, to help them
to further contemplate the possibilities and challenges of developing the
attitudes, knowledge, skills, and dispositions necessary to work effectively with
populations of students who are different from themselves.

IDEOLOGICAL BECOMING

In essence, teacher education programs need to help teachers think reflectively,
introspectively, and critically about issues of diversity. For many developing
teachers, this requires methodologies that help them critically examine their
worldviews or ideologies concerning diversity. These can be obtained by exposing teachers to new ideas, perspectives, theories, and discourses about teaching students from diverse racial, ethnic, and language groups. As they are
exposed to these new perspectives and as they write reflectively about them,
teachers will become aware of the consequences of illiteracy and the discrepancies between their long-held views about teaching, learning, and diversity
and the new ideas they encounter. According to Bakhtin (1981):

> One's own discourse and one's own voice . . . will sooner or later begin to lib-
> erate themselves. . . . This process is made more complex by the fact that a
> variety of alien voices enter into the struggle for influence within an individual's
> consciousness. . . . All this creates fertile soil for experimentally objectifying

another's discourse. Fertile soil for facilitating an ideological struggle that needs to occur, a struggle that will result in more inclusive attitudes toward diversity. As these teachers begin to think critically and change their worlds . . . they are able to encourage their students to do the same. (p. 348)

According to Bakhtin, as teachers begin to liberate themselves from old perspectives or discourses that struggle for influence within their consciousness, then fertile soil will be created for objectifying other discourses. Looking at the processes of teachers' ideological change from a Bakhtinian perspective can help us to conceptualize methodologies that foster the empowerment of teachers to become change agents in our schools.

Through frequent writing assignments, I placed the teachers in ideological positions that challenged them to struggle with critical issues related to teaching, learning, and diversity. Through writing, teachers were given opportunities to critically examine multiple theoretical perspectives and best practices and to consider them in light of their own goals for teaching. I used writing as the primary mode of inquiry that provided critical pedagogical opportunities for teachers to reflect, pose questions, and interrogate their own pedagogies, practices, and philosophies about teaching, and to engage them in the process of ideological becoming. The beginning stages of this process can be heard in the voices of two teachers, Monica and Niko.

DEVELOPING INTERNALLY PERSUASIVE DISCOURSES

Monica was a middle-class, African American student in her early 20s who participated in a teacher education program that was offered at a major university located in the midwestern region of the United States. Monica's writing contained a great deal of reflection, introspection, analysis, and critique as she shared her journey of coming into her own.

When Monica read McElroy-Johnson's (1993) article on issues of voice, she was moved to reflect introspectively on her early educational experiences. Her reading of Freire (1970) gave her the opportunity and the language to critique the existing pressure for non-Whites to conform in this society:

In terms of dialogue and voice, I felt the readings for this week were great for helping me to understand how a person's experience can have a serious influence on their dialogue or how they interpret others' dialogue. I really identified with Beverly McElroy-Johnson's account of feeling "voiceless" because as a child I can remember having a difficult time finding my own sense of identity within a majority-White neighborhood and elementary school. I can also identify with being identified as being "different from other Blacks" because of the way I was raised, and the way I was perceived by Whites throughout grade school. Looking back over my life, I can say that how one is raised definitely has an influence on what "doors will be open to you" and how difficult it will be for you to be successful in society. I agree with Freire that there is a hegemonic dialogue existing in America, where non-Whites feel they have to "conform" in order to succeed, because I know for myself, I had to "play the game" to get to where I am today.

These course readings succeeded in stimulating thoughtful reflection on Monica's part, and she became ever more introspective as she engaged in critique and analysis of the articles and the issues they raised. As she focused on a reading about life in a high school classroom, she noted:

[The article] was great to read, and, unfortunately, I can relate to the teacher. I can remember times, when I gave lessons much like this teacher did, without realizing what kind of effect it has on the students. You know, reading this article allowed me to do a kind of a self-critique, because I kept asking myself: Have you taught this way? Did you ask questions like the teacher? How did I react to students who didn't seem to grasp a concept that was taught previously?

Perhaps if more teachers could see themselves as the topic of discussion in the articles they read and could take the critique and suggestions personally, a reform movement would quickly sweep the globe.

After reading both the Anyon (1981) article about social class and school knowledge and the Delpit (1988, 1992) articles on educating other people's children, Monica wrote in ways that reflected changing ideologies that were being forged through analytical, critical, and reflective writing:

I think these are crucial articles to study when analyzing schools because they discuss issues that I have found to exist in both large and small, private and public schools today. . . . I used my past experiences in public middle- and lower-income areas to critique the author, and I found Anyon to be right on target. . . . Her research seemed to be valid as far as I was concerned, because I found her research to reflect accurately not only on the schools I attended, but schools in which I have observed.

In her own words, Monica attests that she is engaging in change. As she points out, the readings have definitely opened her eyes and given her a critical eye in her viewing of the schools and classrooms that she could potentially be working in. By the second half of the course, Monica's discourse began to show clear evidence of her ideological becoming:

> I find it amazing that after only 1 year of studying . . . I look at education so differently than I did before. When I did my student teaching . . . I had the mindset that if teachers, parents, and students worked together, tremendous changes could occur not only within schools, but also within society as whole. Although I still hold this belief, I now know that it will take more than just teachers, parents, and students working together. I have learned . . . that many schools are purposefully structured to benefit those who come from middle- and upper-income levels, and have been found to hinder others who come from disadvantaged environments.
>
> All in all, I can say my discourse towards education is one that is highly skeptical of the traditional educational system that has been established in this country for many years—this is due to the injustices that I have learned about. . . . I have learned to critique theorists when they make suggestions about educational policy and structure, and judge for myself whether or not their proposals are worthy of consideration by me as an educator.

For Monica, the writing that took place allowed her to step back and see the broader picture such that she could look at her own changing perspectives and see that she now "look[ed] at education so differently than I did before." She even analyzed her own changing mindset over time and spoke of her ability to critique theory, policy, and school structures and to judge their usefulness for herself. The reflective and autobiographical writing that took place in our course provided opportunities for her to connect past, present, and future experiences with the new information she encountered in the class. This allowed her to generate new ideas and strategies for teaching through analysis, critique, and synthesis of the ideas with which she engaged.

As Monica is experiencing ideological change, she is beginning to make plans of action for her teaching. The introspection, critique, and analytical writing that she engaged in moved her to take a stance based on her emerging ideologies. Her ideological growth became more apparent to even her:

> Along with my evolving critique of the educational literature, I think I have developed a level of sensitivity to the needs of students from diverse racial, ethnic, and language groups. I really did not realize how complex teaching could be! I now know that teaching requires more than just preparation from a teacher education program and a

couple of student teaching experiences. I truly think that teaching is an ongoing learning process, where educators need to constantly reevaluate the needs of their students to see if they are being met in the classroom. I think that will be my biggest challenge as an educator, because as I get older, I am sure my classroom will become more diverse and I will need to continue to reassess my teaching style so that I can be as effective as possible.

As she became clearer about the internally persuasive discourses that she would take as her own, Monica began to develop specific plans of action that were an outgrowth of her ideological becoming. She said that she wanted "to try peer learning, cooperative learning, and other alternative approaches, because I want education to become relevant to the students." She extended her analysis and critique in her discussion of whole-language versus skills-based learning, an issue that she had been very interested in since her undergraduate years. She noted that Vygotsky's theory of using constructivism in the classroom is, in her opinion, essentially the basis of whole language. She commented:

> Although I agree with many of the things that whole language claims to do, I do have some reservations with teaching with a totally whole-language approach. I think that it is essential that children learn the skills associated with reading, writing, and speaking. . . . I think that skills should be taught in conjunction with whole-language approaches, so that students are not only learning vocabulary through context clues, but they are also able to spell words or identify them in an isolated format.

In her critique of whole language, Monica is reminded of a school where she volunteered in which "children who were not taught the skills associated with reading and writing in the primary grades were having a difficult time learning new words or words which are pronounced differently than they are spelled." Because of her readings, her observations, and her own teaching and learning experiences, Monica has concluded that "this is why I believe that literacy skills *must* be taught in connection with constructivist learning, because in the end I think it will benefit those children who have difficulty in reading or spelling."

In addition to these decisions about the practice of teaching, Monica has made some critical ideological decisions that will guide her future practice.

> Before I read about the theories presented in our readings for this week, I truly thought that the best way to develop literate learners

was basically to teach them the skills to reading and writing—word recognition, phonics, decoding, etc. . . . I really did not look at teaching reading and writing as a process that could be truly expanded creatively, because I felt that in order to read, students basically needed to learn and know the rules of reading and writing— I thought the drill/practice method would be the most effective.

Well, after learning about the different theories, I now have a new mindset towards literacy. I think I agree most with Vygotsky, and his constructivist approach. I can see the benefit of using scaffolding, because I think that is how all of us learn. We don't really learn best by just being exposed to a lot of material at once. I think we truly learn and remember information when we can relate it to some prior learned information—at least, that is how *I* learn best! I also agree with the "zone of proximal development," because I have witnessed the process of students going from having somewhat of a grasp on information, but later taking what they have learned to a higher level once they have the basic idea. I think that is the ultimate challenge for educators. To constantly monitor their students to see what level they are at, and hence, to adjust their instruction so that the students are constantly being challenged with information that is too difficult for them to do on their own, but with help, they have little or no problem grasping ideas.

I can see myself really getting into a tight spot if I don't take the time to plan and constantly reevaluate my teaching, because students learn at different levels and degrees. However, I think it can be done, and I plan to try to incorporate constructivism within my classroom in the future, by using journal writing, student self-evaluation, and/or portfolios of student work.

For Bakhtin, the process of ideological becoming is made more complex by the fact that competing voices struggle for influence in our teachers' developing sense of consciousness. However, this creates fertile soil in which teachers can objectify and struggle with the various voices and then come to a conclusion about the voices that will eventually influence their own ideological stance. Both Vygotsky and Freire have had a strong influence on Monica's ideological becoming.

I agree with Freire that changes in societal standards of discourse will truly require a change in society; this is no easy task, and I believe it will take someone like Mahatma Ghandi or Martin Luther King, Jr. to change society for the good of all. However, as an educator, I will do my part to try to make sure that all of my students will not only have a "voice," but feel comfortable and not ashamed of where they come from and how they have been raised. I think that educators can at least make their classroom a place where diversity can not only be respected but also appreciated, and that requires the acceptance of *all* student's "voices." Although I may not be able to change society as a whole (as Freire suggests), I can at least make the "minisociety" within my classroom one where various discourses can be shared, and hopefully, do my part to make the voices of my students heard and, most importantly, respected.

Monica's writing exemplifies a teacher's use of reflection, introspection, analysis, and critique as she engaged in the process of ideological becoming. It is interesting to note that she had not been required to exercise these skills very often in her prior teacher education courses.

Niko was an Asian American student who came from a middle-class community in the midwestern United States. Because of the structure of the course, instances of written reflection, introspection, analysis, and critique occurred frequently for Niko as well. Niko's full developmental history is described in Ball (2000); the excerpts below are included here to illustrate how Niko used reflection, introspection, analysis, and critique as she engaged in the process of ideological becoming. Several of those instances deserve to be highlighted. For example, Niko critiqued Delpit's article and used writing to reflect on how it personally challenged her:

> The article by Delpit (1988) was an extremely powerful article that challenged me personally and opened my eyes to the reality and possible struggles that I will potentially have in the future. . . . Delpit's conclusion that "it is impossible to create a model for the good teacher without taking issues of culture and community context into account" (p. 37) is very relevant. . . . As teachers . . . we need to take heed to the possibilities that the problems may reside in ourselves and not in the student. In any case, the responsibility to teach them (not only accept them) is the ideal that we need to instill in ourselves. . . . As I thought about how my readings inform my teaching, the idea that grabbed me most intensely was the idea that we need to "turn ourselves inside out, giving up our own sense of who we are, and being willing to see ourselves in the unflattering light of another's angry gaze" (p. 46). More than applying this to teaching, this is something that should be applied to any and every situation.

As Niko wrote about the theory she encountered, she contemplated theoretical issues related to teaching for diversity, and as she struggled to implement these theoretical notions in her teaching projects and activities, she voiced her changing perspectives in the language she used in classroom discussions, her daily journals, and her reflective essay writing.

> I came into this course arrogant and self-assured. Critical thinking had always been my forte; it has been my natural disposition to try and search for deeper meaning and deeper truths.
>
> I began with my personal essay about . . . "what I wanted to do for the rest of my life." And in this way I began the course, with a love for literature, arrogance from acquired knowledge, and hope for a glorious future. . . . Our class had engaging discussions on critical thinking, on critical reading, communicating with students, and lots of activities. And then I read an article . . . [and] I began to ask lots of questions. . . . And from then on, my arrogance began to deflate. I began to realize my potential role within these students' lives. I was introduced to things I had never even considered. . . . The readings I have done for this class have elucidated cobwebs of half thoughts and have furnished solutions that had begun in my head. . . . In this way my thinking has evolved. . . . Analyzing potential results, and choosing what to incorporate . . . into my future practice as a teacher, . . . I am anxious. . . . I am afraid to make the wrong moves just as I am excited to make the right one. But in the end, I take my future position . . . as a privilege to have the opportunity to help mold the wet clay that will one day become fine art.

As Niko engaged with the theory, readings, and course activities through writing, she began to challenge her prior thoughts about teaching, learning, and diversity. But in the end, she shows evidence of coming into her own as she notes "I take my future position . . . as a privilege to have the opportunity to help mold the wet clay that will one day become fine art." Her discourse indicates that the course activities served as powerful catalysts that influenced her ideological becoming and helped her to seriously consider the challenges of teaching students from diverse racial, ethnic, and language groups. For Niko, the process of coming into her own entailed a critical examination of her own worldview. Evidence of her coming into her own—her ideological becoming—was clearly heard in her emerging voice: "I do not see myself as an English teacher, but a teacher of life, an educator of human emotions, of human relationships, and human history."

Niko's discourse began to change as she became more metacognitively aware of a wide range of perspectives on literacies and teaching and as she reflected on commitment and generative ideologies concerning diversity and educational practice. This process was facilitated through her writing. As she shares her voice, she illustrates some of the ways teachers use language to reveal their evolving ideologies—as they make conscious decisions to become more effective teachers who plan to encourage their students to express their opinions and voices and to become independent workers and critical thinkers.

According to sociocultural theory, human thought is constructed during the dialectic between instruction and development, with *instruction* defined as any directive that elicits activity and *development* as the reorganization of consciousness through that activity. For Monica and Niko, new thoughts and perspectives were constructed during their engagement with the reflection, introspection, analysis, and critique that was facilitated by the use of writing as a pedagogical tool in my course. These new thoughts and perspectives served as a catalyst to help them consider broadened possibilities for their teaching.

Leont'ev emphasized the notion that intellectual activity, such as engagement with theory in teacher education programs, is not isolated from practical activity, which includes ordinary daily activity as well as activities that are generally counted as intellectual. In the cases of Monica and Niko, the intellectual activity was fostered through writing coupled with such interactive classroom activities as discussions, tutoring, class simulations, and I-Searches (first-person accounts of doing a research project using nonprint sources, such as personal interviews), which served as a catalyst for motivating them to develop new action plans for better teaching.

In this chapter, I have drawn on data consisting of written texts produced by two U.S. teachers to provide examples of the reflection, introspection, and critique that emerged in their work as they began to come into their own. I began by arguing that presenting this information could help us better understand the kinds of activities that need to occur in teacher education programs intended to help teachers acquire the attitudes, knowledge, skills, and dispositions necessary to work effectively with students from diverse racial, ethnic, and language backgrounds. In my work with them, I looked for indicators of a developing sense of efficacy on the part of these teachers— the eventual articulation of specific action plans and strategies that they intended to implement in their classrooms—as an important indicator of developing voice and developing commitment. These were indicators that they were coming into their own—seen in their own voices, their own commitments, their own professional selves as teachers of diverse students. Since *commitment* is defined as "the act of taking on the charge, obligation, or trust to carry out some action or policy" and "to make a decisive moral choice that involves a person in a definite course of action" (Webster's Third New International Dictionary, 1986), I looked for my teachers to begin taking on the charge, obligation, or trust to carry out some action. I was pleased to learn of Monica's plans to reassess her teaching style continually, to use peer learning, cooperative learning, and other alternative approaches to make school and learning exciting. I was also pleased about her developing commitment to do her part to try to make sure that all her students had a voice, felt comfortable, and were not ashamed of where they came from, and to create a "minisociety" within her classroom where various discourse could be shared and respected. I was likewise pleased to learn of Niko's plans to look deeply within herself and to consider her future position as a place of privilege from where she could "help mold the wet clay that will one day become fine art."

The reflection, introspection, analysis, and critique that took place in these teachers' writing played an important role in helping them develop broadened perspectives, more inclusive attitudes, and the knowledge and skills needed to teach students from diverse racial, ethnic, and language groups. Through their use of writing as a pedagogical tool, teachers were given numerous opportunities to consider new perspectives and to liberate themselves from old authoritative discourses that struggled for influence within their consciousness. Theory and practice can only be advanced through writing and through teachers' practical experiences with students from diverse racial, ethnic, and language groups, in addition to classroom tutoring and teaching opportunities within a supportive, yet challenging, learning context.

Many teacher education programs, both nationally and internationally, simply expect developing teachers to "swallow the party line" and do as they are told. And some teachers actually *want* to be told exactly what to do. As Bakhtin says, "The authoritative word demands that they acknowledge it, that they make it their own; it binds them." In many programs, the prescribed authoritative discourse demands unconditional allegiance.

This was not the case in my course. Quite the contrary: Through personally challenging their prior beliefs about diversity, I expected teachers to use each reflective, introspective, and critical-writing opportunity to challenge the authoritative discourses that were not serving the needs of diverse populations. For Bakhtin, there is a struggle constantly being waged within the individual to overcome the official line, a struggle against various kinds and degrees of authority. Also according to Bakhtin, when thought begins to work in an independent, experimenting, and discriminating way, what first occurs is a separation between one's own internally persuasive discourse and authoritarian enforced discourse, along with a rejection of those discourses that do not matter to us. However, when we do come into contact with discourses that matter a great deal to us, what occurs is a newly emerging internally persuasive discourse—as opposed to those that are externally authoritarian. And as these internally persuasive discourses are affirmed through assimilation, they become tightly interwoven with "our own words"—our own voices. In the everyday development of our consciousness, our internally persuasive discourse is partly ours and partly someone else's. For the teachers with whom I worked, a part of this consciousness developed as a result of their engagement with new theories, perspectives, and practices in my course. Another part developed as a result of the teachers' own personal reflections, introspections, critique, and personal experiences. The creativity and productiveness that emerged as a result of the introduction of these perspectives consisted precisely in the fact that the exposure to these new discourses awakened new and independent words within these teachers; these discourses helped them to organize their own words from within.

As Bakhtin (1981) remarks, the new words—these new voices that students are introduced to—do not remain in an isolated and static condition. Our old perspectives are reevaluated, and through reflection, introspection, and critique, they are "freely developed, applied to new material and new conditions; and [they] enter into interanimating relationships with new contexts" (p. 346). Thus, fertile ground is created where new perspectives and new discourses can emerge. These newly emerging discourses, which represent the teachers' developing consciousness, become their own as the teachers populate them with their own intentions. This "making it one's own" is the process of ideological becoming. It is the process of coming into one's own. Teacher education programs can facilitate this process through the use of writing as a pedagogical tool and through strategically planned course activities, as I have described here. In the chapter that follows, the voices of three more teachers are examined as these teachers move, not only through the processes of increasing metacognitive awareness, where they are *awakened to new light*; not only through the process of ideological becoming, where they begin to *come into their own*; but also as the process of internalization becomes clearly evident—a process I liken to *teaching eagles to fly*.

Teaching Eagles to Fly:
Facilitating the Emergence of Voice, Advocacy, and Efficacy

Sharing the Voices of Nomha, Jim, and Irene

TEACHING EAGLES TO FLY

Far in the distance, I can barely make out the images of three baby ea-glets. Nearby, the parent eagles are hovering over them with a watchful eye. I can see that they have built their nest near the top of a tall pine tree—in a place of safety. The nest had been lined with very soft feathers, and there, the mother laid her eggs. Almost 12 weeks ago, the eggs hatched and the baby eaglets were born. The babies have been provided all the food and stimulation they need to become healthy and strong. Since there is more than one eaglet, they've become playmates. They play games of tug-of-war, you chase me—I chase you, and broad jump from one side of the nest to the other. Their toys are feathers, sticks, and left-over pieces of lunch that the mother has provided as scaffolds so the eaglets can learn the survival skills they will soon need. For the past 12 weeks, the mother eagle has given them all of her attention, bringing them food regularly, keeping the nest clean, and protecting them. This loving care continues for weeks, and then the time comes when the mother instinctively realizes the eaglets are ready to fly on their own. There is a change in the mother eagle's behavior. She begins to deconstruct the nest—to remove the scaffolds—and she pushes the eaglet to the edge of the nest, and then over the edge! It is the first time the eaglet has used its wings in this manner, and at first it panics and begins to fall to the ground. The mother flies under the frightened eaglet and catches it on her wings. She flies up again, but not back to the nest. She flies high enough and then tips the eaglet off. She does this again and again until the eaglet can fly without help, and it does not return to the nest. She then repeats this process with all the eaglets, until the nest is empty. The eagle knows that if the eaglets stay in the nest they will never spread their wings and learn to fly on their own.

D EVELOPING TEACHERS in teacher education programs are like baby eaglets in many ways—they are exposed to new theories and best practices, but within the context of a caring and supportive teacher education environment. If the learning environment is successfully established as a safe zone, teachers can take risks as they write, discuss, and experiment with new ideas and practices because they feel safe. Sometimes they feel so safe that they do not want to move into the real world of teaching in diverse classrooms—and particularly not in underresourced schools that serve poor and underachieving students. Sometimes they make excuses, saying, "I just don't think I'm the best person to be teaching them. I've decided that I want to teach near my own home, in my own neighborhood. I don't feel prepared at this time. I've decided to teach in a more affluent school for a few years, then, maybe I'll be ready to teach in the more challenging schools." But a good teacher educator knows that teachers need to grow, to develop their own professional voices, to come into their own, to spread their wings to fly. That is why she or he engages them in activities that help them develop a metacognitive awareness of literacy in their lives and in the lives of others. She or he uses writing as a pedagogical tool that promotes reflection, introspection, analysis, and critical thinking—realizing that in order to be effective teachers in challenging schools, they will need to soar, intellectually and in the use of sound practices. You see, eagles don't just fly, they soar. They wait for the right wind to come along, spread their wings, and soar high in the sky. Often they do not need to flap their wings; they simply allow the wind to work for them. And when storms appear, eagles just tilt their wings upward as they continue to soar, because if they tilted them down, the elements would beat them to the ground.

Just as Bakhtin has warned us, getting out of the nest and flying like an eagle is not a seamless process for the eaglet—it requires struggle. The security of the teacher education program and the comforting thoughts of teaching in more affluent schools are like the eagle's nest. They are comfort zones. However, if developing teachers want to become successful teachers of students who are poor, marginalized, underachieving, and culturally and linguistically diverse, they must, at some point, spread their wings and fly on their own. That is to say, they must find their own voices, they must develop a sense of personal efficacy and advocacy, and they must be challenged to develop a commitment to teach students from diverse racial, ethnic, and language groups while still in the comfort zone of the teacher education program. They can be exposed to the theories and ideas of others, but at some point they must begin to come into their own. Just as the mother eagle properly nourishes the eaglet and then, at some point, begins to deconstruct the nest, the teacher educator must first challenge preservice teachers to consider new perspectives, to question past preconceived notions about diversity within a supportive environment; and then she must begin to remove the scaffolds so teachers can develop their own voices. Teachers and teacher educators must look to the future, not to past practices. They must discard unsuccessful practices, misconceptions, and preconceived notions of the inabilities of culturally and linguistically diverse students. When developing teachers have been exposed to sound theoretical perspectives and best practices; have engaged in writing as a pedagogical tool for critical and generative thinking; have worked with students from diverse racial, ethnic, and language groups; and struggled with issues of diversity, whether they realize it or not, they are ready to try their wings and to soar if given the proper support.

Just as eaglets begin their journey with a very limited perspective, developing teachers enter teacher education programs with a limited vision of whom they will be teaching. Through much nurturing—and quite often through much struggle—good teacher educators can prepare these teachers to leave the nest and enter the realities of teaching in a diverse society. Unless these teachers are first properly prepared and then pushed from the nest (with the promise of being provided adequate support), most newly credentialed teachers will fail in their efforts to teach in schools that serve students from diverse racial, ethnic, and language groups.

In this chapter, I introduce the voices of three focus teachers who provide evidence that they are gaining a readiness to fly like eagles—a readiness to be pushed from the nest. Their stories, reflections, and critiques reveal the processes of their developing commitment and sense of empowerment they experienced as they contemplated becoming change agents in schools. These teachers provide support for the argument set forth by McElroy-Johnson (1993) when she says that teachers cannot help students to develop voice unless they develop a voice of their own. In this chapter, I share the voices of two South African and one American teacher in an effort to document the process of moving beyond increased metacognitive awareness and beyond ideological becoming to internalization.

INTERNALIZATION

As explained in Chapter 4, internalization is a concept that emerges from sociocultural theory. It is the social process by which an external social activity (such as observing master teachers as they teach or parroting answers back on a course exam) becomes an internal individual activity or plane of consciousness (such as taking personal ownership of concepts related to diversity, making a personal commitment to effectively teach diverse students, or making issues of diversity a part of one's internally persuasive discourse). As the teachers described in Chapter 5 engaged with theoretical perspectives; challenging discussions; reflective, introspective, and critical writing; and strategically designed curricular activities, they were "awakening to new light," and noticeable changes were detected in their discourses and ideologies concerning teaching students from diverse racial, ethnic, and language groups. The teachers described in Chapter 6 experienced a process of coming into their own through reflection, introspection, and critique. Later, the teachers engaged in teacher research projects that required them to apply the theory that was becoming internally persuasive for them within the context of work with students from diverse backgrounds. As they engaged in these projects, teachers moved beyond the production of seemingly appropriate communication about theory and practice toward an internalizing and synthesizing of ideas. This internalizing and synthesizing of ideas through practice led to an increased sense of efficacy and empowerment for the teachers. The discourse that emerged after the implementation of their teacher research projects provided me with a bridge that I could use to monitor their process of change. (See Ball, 1999, for an extensive discussion of this process.)

In this chapter, I have drawn on an analysis of the literacy histories, oral language, and reflective journal entries of three individual participants in my teacher education course, to illustrate the changes these teachers went through as they internalized theory and then moved beyond internalization to positions of personal commitment and efficacy.

As a result of these engagements, information that was once represented on an external level (the theories and teaching strategies of others) began to take on personal meaning for the teachers. It became an important part of these teachers' internally persuasive discourse (Bakhtin, 1981), which interacted with their prior perspectives to create newly formed perspectives. As Leont'ev (1981) notes, this "process of internalization is not the transferal of an external activity to a preexisting, internal 'plane of consciousness': It is the process in which this plane is formed" (p. 57). Internalization, then, is the process of coming to understand something independently of someone else's thoughts or understandings. It is coming to understand a concept in one's own mind and assimilating it so it will become a part of one's own worldview. When one has internalized something, one can go beyond the initial theory, idea, or activity and beyond one's own previous levels of functioning to expand upon the concept, to relate it to new situations, and to act upon one's own understanding with personal conviction and efficacy. I refer to this process as teaching eagles to fly.

The voices of the teachers that follow demonstrate how in many cases it is possible to observe aspects of the process of internalization through teachers' changing oral and written discourse practices over time and through the reflections they share. It is important to note that the voices of these teachers also support the notion that a teacher education course *can* make a difference in teachers' development when writing as a pedagogical tool for learning is used over time to combine sound theory and practice in the context of teacher research projects that require teachers to work closely with students from diverse racial, ethnic, and language groups.

CREATING SPACES FOR THE EMERGENCE OF VOICE

In one of my courses, which focused on using literacies in strategic ways to effectively teach content area materials to students from diverse backgrounds, my attention was drawn to Nomha, a particularly reticent Black South African female student. As the course progressed, it became apparent that Nomha was developing a readiness to fly on her own. She had been somewhat timid and unsure in her earlier presentations before the class. But during her final presentation of her teacher research project, Nomha stood before the class, hesitated for a moment, and took a deep breath. She then placed her hand on her hip—as a gesture to boost her confidence—looked us directly in the eyes, and said, "OK . . . I'm just gonna tell you exactly what's on my mind." She went on to make an outstanding presentation on the teacher research project she had completed. By the end of the course, she had developed plans of action with extended discussion about ways to tap into the rich cultural and linguistic resources her students brought into the classroom. She had developed strategies that would allow her students to write and speak their ideas and feelings into the curriculum. As Nomha put it, "This course . . . brought back my confidence as a teacher. . . . I have learned so much. . . . I feel as if I am born again. . . . I have changed the direction of my teaching."

What caused Nomha to change? The reflective analytical writing that took place in our course played a critical role in the process of Nomha's coming into her own, and the completion of her teacher research project served as a catalyst that readied her to fly on her own. In what follows, I trace the evolving discourses that show evidence of her internalization and plans for practice through her personal narratives, reflections on the course readings, and discussions of how her participation in course activities influenced her teaching practices.

Nomha began the course by sharing the narrative thoughts that served to increase her metacognitive awareness of her own literacy experiences:

I started my schooling at a lower primary township school in Guguletu.

When reading, we had to repeat after the teacher even if we were saying things that we did not understand. What I liked most at school was to do recital and singing, because I was good at it. I remember one day, however, when I first learned the Lord's Prayer. When I was doing Grade 1, we didn't know what the words were, but we had to sing them in English anyway. There was a part that we sang like this: "Hallow there, give us Lo our Daddy Bre." We were not corrected. We just sang that until I realized that it was not correct in church one day. Most of the time we were taught to memorize without meanings, especially when we were doing our English and Afrikaans lessons. What made learning then not to be fun, was the use of corporal punishment.

As Nomha said, she attended school in a Black South African township where teachers were rigid and quite strict. However, she concludes, "I had fun when I learned." Unfortunately, these early literacy experiences laid a negative foundation for her perception about what it meant to be a teacher as well as her later decision to become a teacher—recitations, memorization, and adherence to rules and punishment. Fortunately, because she had fun when she learned, she decided to become a teacher.

When contemplating their autobiographies of early literacy experiences, participants in my course showed evidence of increasing their level of metacognitive awareness. Statements that began with such phrases as "I could never understand why," "Now I realize that," "I remember one day," "In retrospect I realize that," and "It is only now that I fully understand and appreciate," served as an indicator that these teachers' levels of metacognitive awareness were increasing. As this occurred, many teachers began to question and challenge some of the long-held perspectives that they may not have been consciously aware of earlier. For Nomha, this autobiographical activity served as a readiness exercise that prepared her for consideration of new and different perspectives and visions for literacy practices in her classroom.

After Nomha shared her personal literacy narrative, she was exposed to assigned readings that were carefully selected to broaden her previously held views on literacy and classroom practice. Exposure to these thoughtfully chosen theoretical readings and practical strategies, coupled with authentic teaching experiences and writing used as a pedagogical tool for inquiry, served as the catalyst needed to motivate generative thinking and concrete planning for her. She shared some of her reactions to the course readings:

In reading Vygotsky, I began to realize that the child's development and requests for information depend a great deal on the teacher. The child needs assistance for her development in learning. As the child is engaged in verbal interaction, she develops the higher thinking abilities of awareness, abstraction, and control. I've also learned that a child should be given an opportunity to learn by himself—not scripted.

After reading these articles, I think that rather than giving pupils "topics" chosen by me, I will let them write about their own topics so as to enable them to write more freely. I will use these ideas in my teaching by changing my strategies for learning how my pupils learn, by allowing the pupils to use their mother tongue as the base so as to make them proficient in reading and learning English, by letting pupils bring their experiences into the classroom so that each and every one should be able to learn from others, and by bringing into my classroom the students' home learning environment by putting charts on the walls, and pictures and certain information relevant for education so as to make the classroom have that learning atmosphere.

After Nomha had opportunities to reflect on how she had been teaching, her written reflections revealed that she was already beginning to make action plans to change her teaching approach.

Nomha's teacher research project involved her in an investigation of the question, Can drama be used effectively in a Black township high school classroom as a tool for getting students personally motivated to write extended texts in both their mother tongue and in the school's dominant medium of instruction? After participating in a workshop that I presented on conducting teacher research, Nomha selected her research question and the methodology she would be using. Through this project, she became passionately involved with her students as they selected current social topics that were affecting the youth within the school's immediate community in critical ways. A few of the topics they focused on included AIDS, child abuse, teenage pregnancy, and students' anxieties about writing in a variety of languages while in school and particularly on high-stakes tests. Nomha assisted these high school students as they conducted research to investigate the topics they had chosen. Then, after writing up their research findings, the students converted that information into dramatic plays, which they presented to several audiences, including their fellow students, school administration, myself, and friends and family from their community. This turned out to be a very successful teacher research project, because Nomha learned a great deal about conducting research, about her students' lives and their concerns, and about the effectiveness of using drama to motivate students to write extensively and passionately about topics that interest them in their own mother tongues and in the schools' dominant medium of instruction. Nomha's writing helped her to forge links between our course readings and her developing identity as a teacher, her continuing commitment to teaching and her emerging thoughts about literacy and multilingualism. In her final essay for the course, in the form of a letter, Nomha, a student who came from a very strict and teacher-centered educational background, talked about the profound effect the course had on her.

Dear Dr. Ball:
Firstly I just want to thank you for coming here to [South Africa]. I hope we will be seeing more of you. The few weeks that I have known you, I have changed totally. I feel as if I am a "born-again teacher," meaning that my old thinking, methods, and strategies of teaching have changed to new ones, especially when I read the article by Au.
    I came here to this course with unanswered questions, which is, how do I deal with multilingualism in the classroom. You have answered them all. I never thought when teaching English to my pupils I should use their first language as the base. According to the old South African syllabus, the head of the department did not allow us to do that. But now my perception has changed.
    And also after reading the article by Vygotsky that has changed my perception about literacy. I used to dictate the work [to my students] all the time. I told the students what assignments to go and do and how to do them. But after I read this article, I told the students to give me some topics to write about. I guide them so they can become independent to work without being guided. . . . As a result of these articles you gave us I began to develop an interest in learning more about teacher research. My interest in teaching was crippled when I was retrenched [laid off from a job] when I started teaching in 1988. I was teaching English Standard 6, when I was told that English should be taught by an English speaker. Eventually, my case was taken up by the teacher's union. They wanted to take the matter to [the] high court. The Department of Education threatened me by saying in the whole Republic of [South Africa], I would never be able to teach again. I dropped the charges, because I liked teaching. I still like it. After 5 months of not teaching, I was employed again. However, since 1988 my self-esteem was taken away. My pride as a teacher was gone. I never had an interest in anything after that incident. I didn't want to improve my teachers' qualification since then, I felt "what was the point." I [feared that I] might be seen as useless again.
    Then I saw an advertisement for this course. I couldn't leave teaching because I know the children need me and I need them. That

was the first step I took—to register for this course—after all I've
gone through. So all in all, this course has brought back my confidence as a teacher . . . because the course deals with problems I
encounter in my classroom. I wish, Arnetha, may God be with me to
get all the support I need to further my education for dealing with the
ways of helping a learner. . . . I will always remember you for the
change you have done in my teaching career. May God be with you
and your family till we meet again.

                                                    With love, Nomha

Here, through introspection and reflection, Nomha comes to an understanding of the external and, more important, the internal struggles she has experienced. Her readings and interaction with other perspectives and internally
persuasive discourses in this course have helped her to understand these experiences and to put them into perspective. To this letter, Nomha added the
following specific plans for teaching. Her plans revealed an emerging voice
and sense of efficacy as a teacher:

For me to be successful in leading the child to the better future, I
should know where he comes from and where he is going to. By
coming from I mean his cultural and social background. . . . Secondly,
the child should be free to express his fears, expectations, and goals
so that I'll know where he's heading to.

    Also . . . I think I should address the issues that make learning
difficult for the child so that my teaching can be effective. For
example, in one of my classes one student could not attend school
regularly because she had to go and work in order to support her
family, and that affected her studies. I called her mother and we
discussed the problem and I suggested some other alternatives for
making money. What was the surprise? The girl's progress improved
not only by coming to school regularly, [but also] I think by seeing
that the teacher is concerned about her. I show an interest in their
lives, and I don't look down on them as they are seen in the location
as "low people."

    I also want to instill a sense of pride in their culture, customs,
and language. I made them see the importance of their language first
so that they can learn the second one after having mastered their first
language. I told them "I'm a Xhosa, I'm also not so good in English,
but I'm better than them, though I am still learning it. So let's learn it
together." By doing that I'm trying to build up their confidence so
that when they read in English no one laughs at each other if one
pronounces the word wrongly.

What has helped me a lot and changed me so much is to realize that a good teacher does not only stick to the curriculum, she explores. One should take some of the student's life experiences as part of their learning.

During the course, teachers considered Tharp and Gallimore's (1988) discussion on teachers' process of internalization. They were asked to relate this chapter to a discussion about teachers' developing their own voice as an indication of having achieved internalization. Jim was a European American math teacher in my course. He was in his early 20s and working on his credential and MA degree in education while teaching full time in an inner-city school. After reading Tharp and Gallimore, Jim shared the following reflection:

> I believe that the only methods and theories I can successfully utilize are those which I have first internalized. To me, internalization can take many forms and have a couple of different applications. Overshadowing all these forms, though, is the simple idea that internalization is making a body of information or various processes an integral part of an individual.
>
> Teaching methods which are to be convincingly introduced to [my] students must be those which *I* actually believe are valuable and those which *I* have a deep understanding of. I would like to focus on internalizing two specific theories in literacy which will directly influence decision making in my instruction. The first will be striving to give voice to the voiceless (McElroy-Johnson, 1993) through building the confidence and self-esteem of every student. And the second will be to help students to bridge societal gaps to be able to communicate effectively in the vernacular of the dominant structure of our society (Gee, 1989).

Jim was impressed by the simple idea that internalization is making a body of information an integral part of an individual—whether that individual is a teacher or a student. This realization solidified his commitment to move beyond the instructional model that he had observed as a high school and college student. Going through this process of reflection and introspection helped Jim to feel confident in his decision to strive to give voice to his voiceless students through building their confidence and self-esteem and to help them to communicate effectively as he prepared them to face the challenges of the real world that awaited them.

As a result of being exposed to readings from Vygotsky (1978), McElroy Johnson (1993), and Gee (1989) and other texts, and having opportunities to reflect on these through writing, to discuss them, to challenge them, and to apply the principles that arose to their teaching and learning, these teachers began to internalize useful information. As a result, their thinking began to broaden. In addition, these teachers began to develop their own personal voices, which reflected their evolving perspectives.

One critical step that I noted in this internalization process was that these teachers no longer simply repeated the information that they had read. Instead, the teachers who internalized the information inevitably began to express their own thoughts and opinions. This was especially noticeable when they discussed their teacher research projects. Jim designed and implemented a project that involved teaching inner-city high school math students about reading graphs and interpreting and finding meaning in these graphs and his looking at the application of this information in the lives of his students. As Jim wrote about this, he began to share other important insights that he was gaining:

> My initial view of literacy was to be able to read a graph to find meaning and then write an interpretation of what is being represented. . . . After being exposed to our course readings, I am coming to realize that to be literate in mathematical situations, one must be able to interpret the materials as well, including graphs, charts, and tables. One must also be able to construct informative reports which call for the interpretation of this mathematical data. This requires making meaning or internalization on the part of the student.
>
> I had a success in statistics class this week which lends itself to this discussion. The topic of our lesson was constructing histograms from the data collected from the environment. After collecting the name and birthdays of everyone in the room on the chalkboard, I labeled the board "Data." Then students constructed a line plot and histogram from this data. The histogram was drawn on another board and labeled "Information." Then I posed the question, "What is the difference between data and information?"
>
> One student began groaning and raising his hand and saying, "Wait, wait, wait." I took this as a positive sign of internalization in progress—of the construction of meaning in progress. I waited patiently and finally it came.
>
> "The data is just facts," said Robert, "and the information is for communicating something meaningful, it is organized." I couldn't have hoped for a response any closer to the textbook definition of this dichotomy. My student had built his idea on his own, right there in my class! The concepts were taking on real meaning.

In a later journal entry, Jim wrote:

> The goal in our schools must be to teach beyond application and
> reach for understanding. To be able to read a graph to find meaning
> and then write an interpretation of what is being represented, this is
> the sort of skill that will be useful again and again. . . . Only a small
> fraction of my students will work with complex mathematics to
> construct informational graphs and tables as part of their adult
> lives. But the majority will be at an advantage when they have the
> ability to read and interpret mathematical information: when they
> are able to question what is being presented and derive their own
> meaning.
>   These skills did not occur to me before as a part of literacy. But
> the readings for this class, and particularly the ethnography "Grow-
> ing Up Literate" (Taylor & Dorsey-Gaines, 1988) has made it clear
> to me that people are required to complete standardized forms and
> use tables and charts in order to meet many of the logistical demands
> of society. There are forms at social services offices, bus tables to
> read, and so on, which were essential to the survival of the very poor.

For Jim, internalization involved the development of a personal voice
on issues related to the teaching and learning of literacy. My observation of
the teachers in my course revealed that when internalization was taking place,
then and only then did the generative thought, innovative and personal voices,
and sense of efficacy begin to emerge: voices that were "their own." As these
teachers populated the words of others with their own intentions and ac-
cents, when they appropriated the words, adapting them to their own semantic and expressive intentions (Bakhtin, 1986), then we had evidence that
internalization was occurring.

As I described in more detail in an earlier work (Ball 1999), Jim's development of personal voice and efficacy was evidence that internal activity was
taking place on the part of the teachers themselves (see also Ball, 1998a).
Before this point in our course, his words had existed in other people's mouths,
in other people's contexts, serving other people's intentions (Bakhtin, 1986).
As Jim experienced the process of ideological becoming, these words became
internally persuasive and meaningful for him and they were now serving his
intentions, his purposes, in his teaching. Jim's written discourse revealed that
he was *taking on* the words of theory, suggesting new practices, and making
them his own—combining the utterances of others with his own utterances.
Through his writing we see that he was experiencing internalization as appropriation (Wertsch, 1985), which is a property of action in which teachers

populate theory and suggest practices with their own intentions as they develop a voice of their own and move from this point to begin generating meaningful activity based on their newly emerging convictions.

Jim's final reflections provide evidence that he was developing a sense of efficacy and plans of action that would influence his teaching:

> Of course, I'd like to think that I am not educating students to merely function at the lower socioeconomic levels of our society. That is why probably the most significant insight which I have gained about literacy in this course is the idea that a certain style of teaching can give "voice to the voiceless." Acquired literacy can give a learner the confidence and skills to verbalize their own thoughts and beliefs. This is a level of empowerment for the individual which I had not considered being teachable. I guess I was taught as a child to question, and to read analytically, but I wasn't aware of a need to educate people in a way which encourages liberation of [their] inner voice.

Irene was an early career elementary school teacher in her mid-20s. She attended a teacher education program at a major university located in Western Cape province, South Africa. She implemented a teacher research project that involved her students in pen pal exchanges to develop their voices and broaden their perspectives on the world. Irene's writing revealed that her teacher research project influenced her growing sense of efficacy and personal voice. In the planning stages of the project, Irene had read McElroy-Johnson's (1993) "Teaching and Practice: Giving Voice to the Voiceless" and noted the following:

> I don't want little robots in my class. [I want] to allow my kiddies to talk, to have the space to experiment, to grow, to think for themselves, to pose questions, then to seek more questions, to look at themselves, to help themselves, to speak out for themselves. I want to free my kiddies from what has been, to allow them to be whatever they want to be. I want my students to develop their voice because I, through a series of lectures in this course, am now once again believing in my own voice.

Irene wanted her students to become independent thinkers and develop their own voice. She was developing a strong sense of efficacy, and despite the failure rate of "Colored" and Black students on South Africa's matriculation exams, she believed that her students had the necessary abilities to succeed. When asked to write an essay about her most meaningful learning experience, Irene indicated that the course was having a powerful influence on her as a teacher and on her learners:

> What I am currently experiencing in this course is my most memorable learning experience. This whole course is having such a profound experience on me; it is changing me socially, emotionally, and intellectually. I've learned that despite "the system," I can and want to change my teaching . . . since joining this course I was instilled with new ideas about my approach to tackle and develop literacy in my class.

Irene's writing revealed that she was developing an increased sense of efficacy and advocacy. She wrote, "I know that as much as I don't want to make waves, waves are a part of the nature of events. Having recognized that I need to make a stand for what I believe literacy is, I am far more relaxed. The frustration has eased." Irene's writing provides evidence of her increased sense of voice, efficacy, and advocacy. Following the completion of her teacher research project, Irene gave a report to the class, stating that the project had been a great success and a rich learning experience.

Early in this chapter, I stated that if the learning environment is successfully established as a safe zone, teachers can take risks as they write about, discuss, and experiment with new ideas and practices—that is, if teachers feel safe. In light of Irene's written reflections, it seems that our teacher education course was successful in establishing a safe zone where she could take risks as she wrote about, discussed, and experimented with new ideas and practices. By the end of the course it seemed that Irene was beginning to realize that the time had come for her to leave the nest of our classroom and of the school that she had been teaching in. A few years after the course had ended, I received a letter from her:

> I have since moved from Cape Town Primary [her prior school appointment]. I left soon after our course ended. In finding my voice in your class, I also found my independence. My former school was a very safe environment, so safe that it would have stifled me eventually. That to me was too dangerous, I could not risk that. . . . That year, I applied for another post and was hired to bring transformation in the school.

As a teacher educator I knew that teachers needed to grow, to develop their own professional voices, to come into their own, to be prepared to spread their wings to fly. That is why I engaged them in activities that helped them develop a metacognitive awareness of literacy in their lives and the lives of others, in teacher research projects with students from diverse backgrounds. That is why I used writing as a pedagogical tool to promote reflection, introspection, analysis, and critical thinking—I realized that in order to be effective teachers in today's schools, they would need to develop the attitudes, disposition, and skills necessary to work effectively with diverse student populations, or the day-to-day challenges could beat them down. Irene wrote:

> The [new] school then was the last bastion of apartheid. It certainly made for an extremely interesting ride. I was right there at the cutting edge of transformation. The children had been exposed to hate and prejudice. . . . But, through hard work, patience, and lots of love, we have brought the children together.

Just as Bakhtin warned, ideological becoming requires some struggle—getting out of the nest and flying like an eagle is not a seamless process for the eaglet. This applied to Irene:

> I am enjoying myself, but I must admit that it is quite stressful. . . . My new school is by no means an easy environment to work in, it is too fraught with prejudice and misunderstanding. I suppose that is to be expected since we are still trying to come to terms and understand all that has happened in this country. [But] it still makes for an interesting learning experience.

However, it is good to know that when teachers have been exposed to sound theoretical perspectives and best practices, have engaged in writing as a pedagogical tool for critical and generative thinking; have worked with students from diverse racial, ethnic, and language groups; and have struggled with issues of diversity, whether they realize it or not, they are ready to try their wings and soar if given the proper support. Irene ended her letter by saying, "One thing is sure. I will never be quite the same after this experience. Thank you for your class!"

Upon entering my course, students were confronted with the challenge of considering these issues through interpersonal and socially mediated forums, including individual and shared reflections on these issues, extensive written engagement with carefully designed prompts on various thought-provoking topics, and discussions that caused them to challenge their preconceived notions on these issues. Exposure to theoretical readings and practical activities took place during the course to serve as a catalyst to engage students in dialogic conversations that could influence their thoughts on issues of diversity. However, engaging teachers in writing that draws on the two major modes—analysis and synthesis—helps them to bring past, present, and future perspectives together. From this broadened perspective, they began to conceptualize the possibilities of teaching students from diverse backgrounds in fresh and exciting ways (Emig, 1977, p. 13). As a result of their engagements in thoughtful and reflective writing, along with their teacher research projects, the teachers were able to bring theory and practice together to crystallize the internalization process. Teaching students from diverse racial, ethnic, and language groups began to take on deeper and more personal meaning for the teachers, and they began to go beyond the initial ideas and activities presented in class. They began to move beyond their previous levels of thinking to expand on the concepts presented in class, relate them to the new situations they engage with on a daily basis, and act on their new understandings with personal conviction. According to one teacher in my class:

> Vygotsky's theory holds that unless a concept is internalized, it is not learned. Internalization is more than a cognitive accomplishment that occurs only "in the head." It also means that the concept becomes a part of the learner.

The research data from this study revealed that in many cases it was possible to observe aspects of internalization through the oral and written reflections shared by the teachers. In the case of the teachers in my course, two forms of evidence support the notion that internalization was indeed taking place: the teachers' development of a personal voice and their movement *beyond* the ideas and activities presented in class as they generated plans of action that reflected their own commitment. In Vygotskian theory, human thought is constructed during activities based on a dialectic between instruction and development, with *instruction* defined as any directive that elicits activity and *development* as the reorganization of consciousness through that activity. For Nomha, Jim, and Irene, new thoughts, perspectives, and commitments were constructed during their engagement with writing and with the activities that took place in my course. These thoughts, perspectives, and commitments served as a catalyst to help them consider broadened possibilities for their teaching. The voices of these three students provide us with insights that help us understand some of the internal activity that goes on as teachers develop philosophies.

Through the teachers' own voices, I have introduced rich illustrations of how increased metacognitive awareness, reflection, introspection, analysis and critique, and engagement with teacher research projects that focus on students from diverse racial, ethnic, and language groups can lead to internalization. These teachers' voices show that internalization can serve as a catalyst for generative thinking and the emergence of voice that are critical in the development of teachers who have the ability and the will to teach students from diverse backgrounds. These encounters gave way to the development of strategies that ultimately evolved into generative plans of action for future teaching. In the following chapter, we learn how these plans of action are transformed into practice and discuss why this final step is so important. The voices of these teachers reveal how the course activities influenced their ultimate development into carriers of the torch.

Carriers of the Torch: A Call to Commitment

Sharing the Follow-Up Voices of Gafumbe, Mosola,
Mieko, Nomha, Monica, Niko, Jim, and Irene

Never doubt that a small group of thoughtful committed people can change
the world: indeed it's the only thing that ever has!
—Margaret Meade

A CCORDING TO THE National Association for Multicultural Education (2003), we are faced with a monumental challenge to prepare a teaching force that has the knowledge, skills, and dispositions necessary to provide multicultural education to *all* students. In other words, we are faced with the enormous challenge of preparing committed change agents—or carriers of the torch—for our schools. Accomplishing that task would be a critical step toward fulfilling the demands described in the following statement:

Multicultural education is a process that permeates all aspects of school practices, policies and organization as a means to ensure the highest levels of academic achievement for all students. It helps students develop a positive self-concept by providing knowledge about the histories, cultures, and contributions of diverse groups. It prepares all students to work actively toward structural equality in organizations and institutions by providing the knowledge, dispositions, and skills for the redistribution of power and income among diverse groups. Thus, school curriculum must directly address issues of racism, sexism, classism, linguicism, ablism, ageism, heterosexism, religious intolerance, and xenophobia.

Multicultural education advocates that students and their life histories and experiences should be placed at the center of the teaching and learning process and that pedagogy should occur in a context that is familiar to students and that addresses multiple ways of thinking. In addition, teachers and students must critically analyze oppression and power relations in their communities, society and the world.

To accomplish these goals, multicultural education demands a school staff that is culturally competent, and to the greatest extent possible racially, culturally, and linguistically diverse. Staff must be multiculturally literate and capable of including and embracing families and communities to create an environment that is supportive of multiple perspectives, experiences, and democracy. Multicultural education requires comprehensive school reform as multicultural education must pervade all aspects of the school community and organization.

Recognizing that equality and equity are not the same thing, multicultural education attempts to offer all students an equitable educational opportunity, while at the same time, encouraging students to critique society in the interest of social justice. (National Association for Multicultural Education, 2003)

This may appear to be a daunting task, but it is not an impossible one. The research that I have completed and reported on in this book can help us to accomplish these goals and in particular that of preparing teachers to become change agents in our schools. This program of reform must involve all the key stakeholders in becoming concerned about the increasing number of traditionally underrepresented individuals who are now competing for scarce public resources and being alert to the subsequent risk of social division.

Teacher education programs that do an effective job of preparing teachers to educate diverse student populations ultimately influence school and community structuring and financing in positive ways (see McDonnell, Timpane, & Benjamin, 2000). In the United States, schools that do not meet accountability standards will lose federal funding as a result of the No Child Left Behind Act of 2002. This kind of public policy has greatly affected schools that currently serve poor, marginalized, and underachieving populations in the United States. Financing schools that serve poor and marginalized students is a major challenge to the South African educational system as well. While we know that globally most student bodies are now segregated, we realize that the teachers in these schools may come from different racial, ethnic, linguistic, or socioeconomic backgrounds from their students—and so teacher education programs should focus on preparing teachers for diversity. But even if teachers do not end up teaching in diverse school environments, they should still be prepared to teach in "sensitizing" ways that help students begin to see themselves as part of a globally diverse society.

Teacher educators should care about today's changing global demographics and the need to prepare teachers for diversity for many reasons. Programs that reflect such an emphasis will inevitably increase their chances of attracting students from more diverse backgrounds into teaching. Students who attend very diverse programs leave schools of education more prepared for society's changing demographics and more ready to address issues that result from those changes—such as the building of diverse classroom communities and the appropriate distribution of classroom, school, and community resources. Well-prepared teachers can improve the quality of students' lives and increase the levels of productive activism on our campuses. This book was written to support the efforts of those who care about addressing these issues.

WHAT WE CAN LEARN FROM THE VOICES OF THE TEACHERS IN THIS BOOK

There are many things to be learned from this research, particularly by listening to the voices of the transformed as well as the nontransformed teachers. First, by listening to the voices of the transformed teachers we gain insights than can be used to begin crafting a nuanced understanding of the lived experiences of students and teachers in underresourced schools. In addition, "interested others" (teachers, teacher educators, administrators, and policy makers) can gain insights from which to craft expanded visions for reforming schools to become equitable learning environments for all students. We can also learn lessons about how to support those who teach and learn there.

Listening to the voices of the transformed teachers in my research, I have learned a great deal that will be valuable to those who are interested in answering the question, How can we structure teacher education programs to facilitate the development of teachers who have the attitudes, knowledge, skills, and dispositions necessary to work effectively with students who are different from themselves? Specifically, I learned how important it was to ground the work of teacher education programs in sociocultural theory. Moreover, I learned that, contrary to popular belief, teachers' engagement with theory in a teacher education course is appreciated and is applied to their teaching practices long after teacher education programs have ended. Listening to teachers is critically important because their voices can provide some of the most convincing evidence of the impact of teacher education programs on their changing perspectives concerning diversity and their changing practices. In the sections that follow, I elaborate on these findings.

The Importance of Sociocultural Theory

Listening to the voices of the transformed and nontransformed teachers in this research, I came to see how important it was that teacher education programs consider potential students' zones of proximal development when selecting candidates to enter their programs. This notion should be considered during preadmission interviews if we are serious about preparing curriculum and course materials that will fall within developing teachers' zones of proximal development. As Cazden (1988) has noted, "It is important not to have a mechanical conception of the process of internalization. . . . [If] overt social interaction . . . [is to become] transformed into covert mental processes . . . [then] the learners [must] somehow figure things out for themselves" (pp. 107–108). Cazden's point here is well taken: Learners must be willing to exert some effort in figuring things out for themselves if they are to benefit from the programs that are offered. Discovering new ideas and going beyond the information that is given to them in the program assumes some effort on the part of learners. Intellectual transformation and internalization are not processes that can be mechanically imposed on students. Students' willingness to exert some effort in figuring things out for themselves and their openness to engaging with what the programs have to offer should be considered important factors during the admissions process.

The stories shared in Chapters 5, 6, and 7 focus on the processes of teacher change as depicted in my model of teacher change (see Figure 4.1). The teachers' evolving ideologies are revealed through their changing discourse practices and their subsequent teaching practices. The eight teachers discussed in these chapters illustrate what can happen when instructional practices fall within teachers' zones of proximal development. As Vygotsky points out, the best instruction occurs when it "proceeds ahead of development," that is, when instruction is presented to a learner when they are willing to consider new notions, when they are willing to contemplate new ideas, and just before they are developmentally ready to embrace those concepts and accompanying best practices. In such cases, the introduction of new information has the potential to awaken those new functions in the learner that are in the process of maturing. This phenomenon was most evident in the cases of the transitioning teachers in my study.

At the onset of the course, these teachers relied almost exclusively on the words, theories, and ideas of others as the primary voice of authority concerning issues of educating diverse students. As the course progressed, they were actively considering and applying new ideas. They used the theory and suggested best practices of others to validate their own emerging perspectives—combining the utterances of others with their own. By the end of the term, these teachers were beginning to move beyond simply parroting the information presented to them in class and they were populating those ideas with their own intentions—adapting them to their own practices, purposes, and intentions (Bakhtin, 1981). On the basis of these observations, I concluded that when instruction occurs within a teacher's zone of proximal development and when they are willing to consider, contemplate, and try out new ideas, perspectives, and practices, then the development of teachers' philosophies can be altered by contact with strategically selected inputs from teacher educators, theoretical readings, and interactions with colleagues when negotiated within the context of reflective, introspective writing and discussions that extend the teachers' zones of proximal development.

Just as sociocultural theory helped to explain the success of my work with many students, it also helped to explain my lack of success with non-transitioning students. Sociocultural theory helps us to understand that the different backgrounds, dispositions, attitudes, and cognitive abilities that students bring to the learning environment will influence the success of teacher education programs in reaching their expressed goals of preparing teachers to work with students from different racial, ethnic, and language groups. If the instruction does not fall within these students' zones of proximal development, it will have little impact on preparing them to teach diverse student populations.

I have pointed out that not all the teachers reacted to my course in the same favorable ways. Some preservice teachers had firm opinions regarding the challenges of teaching diverse students and these opinions changed either very little or not at all during my course. From the students' writings and the discussions that occurred in the classroom, I deduced that some teachers started the course with a commitment to issues of diversity, and their commitment seemed to become more evident throughout the term. Some transitioning teachers started the course without a commitment to the issue of diversity and they displayed evidence that a commitment was developing as the course proceeded. Some teachers started the course without a commitment to issues of diversity and did not appear to change their attitudes over the course of the term. The analysis of the data showed that among the American teachers, approximately 26% had been committed to teaching poor and marginalized students before the course began, 44% percent were transitioning teachers who began to seriously consider teaching these students as a result of the course, and about 30% had not been committed to teaching students from diverse racial, ethnic, and language groups before the course began and were not after it ended. Among the South Africa teachers, approximately 30% had been committed to teaching poor and marginalized students before the course began, 48% were transitioning teachers, and 22% had not been committed to teaching students from diverse racial, ethnic, and language groups before the course began and were not after it ended.

Some might look at these figures and say the course was a failure because it did not result in a transformative experience for all the teachers. However, I look at these figures and say that if only the 44% to 48% transforming teachers in our teacher education programs show a favorable change toward diversity as a result of our courses, this work is a success and is critically important because our courses have succeeded in effecting transformation in a large percentage of teachers, who might otherwise have left their teacher education programs without developing a commitment to or seriously contemplating the rewards of teaching diverse students. While not all preservice teachers showed the degree of commitment and transformation that I might have desired, all the teachers gained the experience of and exposure to inclusive perspectives, pedagogical approaches, and content knowledge that provided a foundation for their later development toward becoming effective teachers of students from diverse backgrounds. Perhaps when given the opportunity and under the right conditions, they too will blossom, at a later date.

The most hopeful and exciting results of this research were found in the transforming teachers who took the course. In this book, I have focused most of my attention on these transitioning teachers because they were receiving instruction within their zones of proximal development. I believe that the information gained from the study of these teachers will be most useful to current reform efforts. In addition, I realize that the information gained from a study of this population of teachers will be most helpful to stakeholders who are seeking an answer to the question, How can we structure teacher education programs to facilitate the development of teachers who have the attitudes, knowledge, skills, and dispositions necessary to work effectively with students who are different from themselves? Such programs must build on Vygotsky's notion that the best instruction occurs when it proceeds ahead of a teachers' development, while they are in the process of maturing. In this way, instruction in teacher education programs will have the greatest potential of awakening teachers to those functions that will be most useful in their work with diverse students. This phenomenon was most evident in the transitioning teachers. I concluded that sharing the voices of these teachers would provide valuable information for teacher education programs that work toward graduating a higher percentage of teachers who are committed to issues of diversity. These teachers showed the greatest potential for helping to fulfill the demands set forth by the National Association for Multicultural Education—for developing a teaching force that is culturally competent, diverse, multiculturally literate, and supportive of multiple perspectives and experiences.

One Course Can Make a Difference

Contrary to earlier studies that found that teachers' practices do not change as a result of teacher education or professional development programs, my research confirmed that one teacher education course can be structured to facilitate the development of teachers who have the attitudes, knowledge, skills, and dispositions to work effectively with students from racially, ethnically, and linguistically diverse backgrounds. In his discussion of the relationship between instructional policy and teaching practices, Cohen (1990) probed important issues of teacher change. After conducting close observations of a teacher he referred to as Mrs. O, he concluded that her changing practices were simply a mélange of novel and traditional material; Cuban (1984, 1986) reported that even teachers who avidly desire change can do little with most schemes to improve instruction, because most of the proposed schemes do not work well in classrooms. Cohen noted that while Mrs. O eagerly embraced change and found new ideas and materials that worked in her classroom, she still seemed to treat new topics as though they were a part of her traditional practices. Although she revised her curriculum, she still conducted her class in ways that discouraged exploration of students' understanding. In contrast, the transitioning teachers in my study encouraged their students' exploration of understanding; critical thinking and student queries were invited; alternative perspectives were welcome; and students were encouraged to explore their own language and literacy practices in ways that signaled innovation, ideological becoming, internalization, generative thinking, and an emergence of the teachers' own personal voices on issues related to diversity. The transforming teachers in my study were cultivating attitudes of curiosity and a willingness to probe and explore cultural aspects of their learning. As they rewove the fabric of social and intellectual life within their classrooms, some old threads were removed from the curriculum, and new ones were added, in meaningful ways. In the closing pages of his essay, Cohen asks, What would it take to make additional, helpful, and useful guidance available to teachers? What would it take to help teachers pay constructive attention to it? As Cohen noted in 1990, with few exceptions (Lampert, 1988; Lee, 1995, 2000, 2001; Popkewitz, 1976; Richardson, 1994; Weisman & Garza, 2002), neither of these queries has been given much attention in the literature. Yet without good answers to these questions, it is difficult to imagine that meaningful changes will occur. In order for them to happen, developing teachers must become engaged with acquiring new ways of thinking about teaching, learning, and diversity over time, and they must construct new practices for operationalizing this new knowledge. This book is a response to Cohen's question, What more might have been done to support Mrs. O's efforts to change?

From the model I presented in Figure 4.1, teacher educators can see that Mrs. O seems to have completed Phase 1 of the model: she has developed an increased metacognitive awareness of the demands of the new curriculum and adapted a few lessons based on that increased awareness. For the deeper kinds of changes that are needed, Mrs. O also needed to experience conceptual and ideological change, a process of internalization, and the development of her own well-informed voice and teacher efficacy that was based on a deep consideration and understanding of sound theoretical principles and a knowledge base grounded in demonstrated best practices. Using writing as a pedagogical tool for reflective, introspective, and critical thinking and completing her own teacher research projects, Mrs. O would stand a better chance of developing her own voice, a sense of efficacy, and plans of action that were grounded in sound theory and best practices.

I shared the written reflections of eight transforming teachers in Chapters 5, 6, and 7 to illustrate how they experienced the first three phases of the model I introduced. Following are some of the concluding voices of these teachers, who ultimately completed the fourth and most critically important phase of the model—that of transforming their plans of action into meaningful practice. I refer to this phase of the process of teacher change as critically important because, as Sleeter (2001a) points out:

> [While] improving students' attitudes and raising their awareness of issues certainly have value . . . it is not the same as producing teachers who are effective in multicultural, high-poverty schools. . . . We need, rather, to focus on preservice teachers' classroom performance in schools in which children of color and children from poverty backgrounds are clustered and to investigate what happens in preservice programs that significantly develops their teaching. (pp. 219–220)

The voices of the teachers that follow show evidence of their changing perspectives concerning literacy and the influence of those changing perspectives on their changing teaching practices over time. Evidence of these changing perspectives comes from the teachers' written reflections, interviews, and follow-up classroom observations, collected between 1996 and 2005.

All the transitioning teachers' definitions of literacy broadened. These broadened definitions expanded far beyond academic reading and writing within the classroom walls. Most of the teachers' definitions grew to include entities in the world that their students encountered on a daily basis. When asked to contribute comments concerning the evolution of her definition of literacy since the end of the course, Mieko responded that "to be literate within the context of our school is to be able to understand exactly what the requirements are." However, she added:

> It's evident that students need to be able to read in the language of instruction. But just being able to understand what's required of them in school is not enough. So they must acquire a certain amount of support, so the literacy that they acquire is related to the skills they will need to survive inside school and inside their community. And that's what we find with a lot of children that are poor.

Gafumbe noted that his definition of literacy "had grown beyond what I thought before because literacy to me now might also mean interpreting technologically for the kids. Literacy now has an added importance to me

because it might mean that you are able to fully utilize what is around you."
Now Gafume realized that

> literacy is not confined to one place or one situation. It is an ever-
> expanding thing. Which means now that people shouldn't confine
> themselves either. . . . Now, can we say that because they cannot read
> or write they are illiterate? Although the term *illiterate* might be
> stemming from being able to read or write, but most people can
> interpret the situations around them, in their environment. And so
> now we're saying that person is literate as well to some extent.

Mosola noted that his definition of literacy had expanded in terms of
understanding literacy as it related to terms such as *globalization*, *govern-
mentalization*, and *high technology*, and how he was beginning to see the
world. Mosola acknowledged his understanding that

> there is the basics of literacy, but then it doesn't just stop there. There
> is another world out there, and how the surroundings out there and
> other people are relating to and understanding each other out
> there. . . . So by coming to understand this, you are becoming much
> more literate. This definition broadens the aspects of literacy beyond
> reading and writing. By being literate, it's for me to I say I have the
> ability to be able to communicate with other people within my
> surroundings. Maybe using forms of writing, maybe orally, and
> obviously now using forms of technology, Internet, and others. All of
> these encompass forms of literacy.

THE INFLUENCE OF ONE COURSE ON PRACTICE

During my initial visits to these teachers' classrooms, I realized that the articulation of specific action plans and teaching strategies that they intended
to implement in their classrooms was evidence that they were beginning to
experience ideological change. Of critical importance, however, was the fact
that I was able to investigate the actual implementation of those plans of
action during my follow-up visits to their classrooms, from 1996 to 2005.
This evidence was particularly important because, as we know, developing
a commitment is defined as "the *act* of taking on the charge, obligation or
trust to *carry out* some action or policy; to make a decisive moral choice that
involves a person in a *definite course of action*" (Webster's Third New International Dictionary, 1986; emphases added). However, acting on that
commitment is the true test of teacher change and transformation. Thus, these

teachers' journeys to becoming carriers of the torch needed to culminate in their acting on the commitment to becoming effective teachers of students from diverse racial, ethnic, and language groups and to become change agents in their schools.

When I returned to observe and interview these teachers I did not expect to see a specific set of strategies or lessons being implemented in their classrooms, because my course was not prescriptive in nature. Instead, the course emphasized attitudes, dispositions, assumptions, and theoretical perspectives that must underlie the teaching practices of teachers who hope to become effective teachers of culturally and linguistically diverse students. It provided teachers with an opportunity to develop their own ideological stances and a sense of efficacy that would form the basis for their ongoing development. Such an ideological stance would guide them in selecting techniques and approaches that would promote the use of higher-order thinking skills on the part of their students. I observed this ideological stance as I watched the teachers encourage their students to explore a deeper understanding of what their textbooks were saying; to use critical thinking about how to respond to writing prompts that were assigned; and to pose queries that challenged the authoritative voices of the teacher, the textbooks, and their peers. I also observed the teachers as they presented alternative perspectives on the topics being covered and as alternative perspectives were invited from the students. And finally, students in these teachers' classrooms were encouraged to explore a deep understanding of the language and literacy practices that they used in their own homes and communities.

My follow-up meetings with Mieko and Niko were held only a few months after the course ended; with Monica, 1 year after the course; with Jim, 2 years following the course; with Gafumbe, Irene, and Mosola, 3 years following the end of our course; and with Nomba, 3 years, 7 years, and 8 years following the end of our course. During my observations of these teachers' classrooms, I witnessed the work of some truly powerful and inspiring teachers who were able to give ongoing attention to integrating issues of language development and language diversity into their lessons. In each classroom I also observed ongoing assessments of the teachers' effectiveness in meeting their students' needs. Some teachers used exit slips at the close of their lessons on which the students told what they learned during the day's lesson. Others began or ended the class with interactive dialogue that informed the teacher of the success or failure of the day's instructional goals. Still others used student portfolios to provide continuing assessment of their students' learning.

Three months after the course ended, I visited Niko's school and observed her classroom of 22 African American and Latino students from low-income backgrounds. Niko exposed all her students to an array of culturally rich materials, reflecting the multiple heritages represented in the school and surrounding community. As she taught her culturally and linguistically diverse students an English literature lesson, she skillfully wove a message of acceptance of the students' culture and their ideas into her delivery of the lesson.

Three months after the course ended, I observed Mieko as she taught a mathematics class in an inner-city midwestern classroom. While her demeanor was low key, she was able to command the respect and attention of every student in the classroom. She motivated them to work persistently and to think deeply about the content even when they wanted to give up. She gave the students lots of one-on-one assistance and regularly stayed after class to provide extra help. Mieko also used writing-to-learn and journal writing in her class to give students opportunities to gain a deeper understanding of the mathematical concepts.

One year after the course ended, my visit to Monica's classroom, in a diverse but middle-class community, highlighted the need to develop sensitivity and skills concerning issues of diversity in all teachers, not just those who would be working in high-poverty schools. Monica incorporated materials that reflected a wide range of perspectives during a social studies lesson on Columbus's "discovery" of America. The students were exposed to the traditional history book version of the story as well as an American Indian point of view. She used a wide range of primary source materials, texts, and multimedia materials in presenting the lesson. In doing so, she succeeded in including historically diverse voices in the lesson as well as the voices of her students who came from varied backgrounds as she drew on narrative and expository texts and the poetry that some of her students had written.

I visited Jim's inner-city math classroom in the United States 2 years after the course had ended and observed him working tirelessly to maintain the focused attention of each of the mostly African American students in his class. Jim's ability to engage all his students—even one who had been labeled as having attention deficit disorder (ADD)—in higher-order thinking skills in a school environment where most of the teachers had abandoned such a goal, demonstrated his commitment, tenacity, and creativity in meeting the targeted goals he had articulated while in my course.

Three years after the course ended, I returned to South Africa and visited Mosola's history classroom in a township high school, which contained about 40 students of color from several different language backgrounds. As I observed the class, I noted that students listened carefully as Mosola introduced new terminology in both Xhosa and English while describing the World War II context for the class discussion. As the lesson progressed, Mosola's classroom struck me as a model intercultural community of exchange. Mosola demonstrated his skillful use of students as translators and interpreters in the class; one by one, multilingual students were called up to the front of the classroom to translate different parts of the lesson in their mother tongue, to increase their struggling classmates' comprehension and retention of the materials that were being taught.

When I visited Irene's classroom 3 years after the course ended, I observed that she was now serving not only culturally and linguistically diverse students but also the children of former prisoners and prison guards who were now learning together on South Africa's famed Robin Island. During my visit, I observed the inquisitiveness of students who were fully engaged with the project-based lesson she was leading. The hands-on nature of the project, the probing discussions, and the writing activity that followed the discussion allowed the students to see themselves and their own experiences in the lesson.

When I visited Gafumbe 3 years after the course ended, he was busily performing the duties of principal at his township school. As he showed me around the school, going from classroom to classroom, the respect and warmth with which he was regarded was apparent. Later that day, when I sat in on a staff meeting that he was conducting, I could hear echoes from our course readings as he advised the teachers to be mindful of their students' struggles in transitioning from the use of their mother tongue to the use of English as the medium of instruction in their classrooms. He listened actively to the teachers, who expressed some frustration in their efforts to implement new strategies in their classrooms, and he offered suggestions about how they could teach lessons more effectively.

Three years after the course ended, I visited Nomha's classroom. There, I observed a class of 40 students engaged in the presentation of dramatic skits that they had composed themselves, using the multilingual scripts that they had written in small groups to address with great passion critical issues such as child abuse, AIDS, and teen pregnancy. The students were totally engaged in preparing and presenting the lessons. As they integrated English and their mother tongue into the presentations, they spoke with a real sense of confidence and purpose. When I visited this teacher's classroom in 2004, the students were performing the powerful skits they had written for the theme "Ten Years of Democracy in South Africa." And when I visited Nomha's classes in 2005, she was busy coaching students who had been selected to represent their school in a formerly all-White oratory competition. I later found out that one of these students won the competition. She was also teaching writing to large classes of students who wrote about the challenges of taking matriculation examinations in a language that was not their mother tongue. She continued to use drama and art to motivate her students to become better writers.

To triangulate these observation data, I conducted interviews with each of the teachers. During these interviews, rich reflective comments emerged.

I found that not only were their classroom teaching practices different as a result of the course, but the teachers' talk was distinctly different as well. My observations indicated that whether the teachers were engaged in discussion with their colleagues, school officials, their students, parents, or me, they now often referred to theory or an ideological stance that guided their teaching, their own experiences, or a deep understanding of the experiences of their students in their conversations. They also spoke with a sense of efficacy that was noticeably stronger than when the course began. My interviews with the teachers were tape-recorded and transcribed following my visits. The tape recordings were supplemented by videotapes of the teachers' classroom teaching, field notes, and photographs that were taken at the time of our interview meetings. All these data confirmed these teachers' movement toward becoming carriers of the torch. I observed them reweaving the fabric of social and intellectual life within their classrooms—as old threads were being removed from the curriculum and new ones were being added.

TEACHERS' APPRECIATION FOR AND APPLICATION OF THEORY

Sleeter (2001a) and others have asked the critical question, Do teachers feel that teacher education courses have had any long-term influence on their subsequent teaching practices? These scholars have called for research that focuses on the teachers' follow-up classroom performance in schools that serve students of color and students from poverty backgrounds. During my follow-up observations and interviews with the teachers in my course, I pursued this question and learned that these teachers saw value in the theory I presented to them and felt that their subsequent teaching was affected by that theory. In my follow-up interviews I asked the teachers, "Looking back, which of the theorists or scholars from the course stand out most in your mind?" and "Which concepts from the course have turned out to be most memorable for you?" Their replies were insightful and very enlightening. The teachers were clearly able to articulate their recollections of the theoretical readings and the long-term influence that they had had on their teaching. Thus, the teachers' engagement with theory in our teacher education course was appreciated and influenced their teaching practices long after the teacher education course ended.

For example, Nomha informed me that the lesson she remembered most from the course was to guide her students to become independent. She stated that this was something she remembered from our conversation about Vygotsky on scaffolding and our conversation about McElroy-Johnson on voice. She noted:

What I did to build on the concept of voice was I let my students write books about their families, their different cultures, the way they do things, and their customs. Even though we are mostly Xhosa speakers in my classes, we practice our customs in different ways. We do things according to our clans. So by writing those books we've learned things that we didn't know about each others' backgrounds and about things that are very important to them. And we managed to write unconsciously, without feeling self-conscious. And then if something is bothering them, it comes out in their writing and using that I was able to help many of them.

Also, what I remember about the course is to bring the language of the students into the classroom and also to consider their background. You'll find in one class, many of the children are not Xhosa speaking only, many speak several languages. And when I teach them, I try by all means to consider where they come from, culturally, and traditionally. . . . And there are not as many restrictions in my class, like using their mother tongue, so they are not afraid to express themselves.

Nomha concluded by saying,

You see. . . . most of the books in our school are written in English and that's hard for the kids. But this book that I like that I'm using now, it's using all different languages though it's also an English book. So what I told my students is, like this book, they too can use any language they like. They will write in English, you know, and then sometimes you will notice that they change to Xhosa and then back to English, and then some in Sesutu, and then after a while they will indicate to me, they'll say "Ma'am, I'd like to write this part in Xhosa." So to them, now the English period is very interesting because they are free to express themselves in their mother tongue. And in this way I find that they write more often and they write longer essays.

Irene recalled that she had been most influenced by the article written by McElroy-Johnson (1993) focusing on giving voice to the voiceless. She vividly recalled learning about the Ebonics controversy in the United States. She noted:

That still stayed with me because the African American/Standard English issues and Afrikaans/English issues are so similar. The whole

1997 issue of Ebonics really shook me and just stuck with me. The similarities of what is happening in our cultures, in our tongues, it's the same things happening in South Africa and the United States, and we'd better find a way to deal with it, otherwise we're going to lose a lot of children.

Recalling her reading of Hudelson (1994) and Bakhtin (1981), Irene discussed the ways in which she had incorporated the idea of multiple literacies into her teaching, which she did because, as she put it, "I remember when we covered this in class, and I said to myself, 'I must never forget this.' And I'm pleased to see that subconsciously it sunk in."

During my follow-up visits with Mosola, he commented that "the most memorable learning experience I remember from the course was your teaching style . . . which I like it very much. You know, sometimes I use those strategies in my classroom." He continued:

What I think I loved most is when we had no wrong answers. And you gave us freewrites. And whatever our ideas were, they were accepted and encouraged and considered right. . . . For me this was the most powerful thing, which I try to use in my classes. I believe in using that very seriously because you are building up the students' confidence, you know, to believe in themselves. . . . And this is exactly what I was doing in my classrooms when you came to visit.

And then, there was this teaching style, this Vygotsky teaching style, of giving support [scaffolding]. I tried this with my students and the kids began to become independent and critical thinkers. But also the support you gave to us at the same time—giving the support so that each person can understand that you are with him or her. So in other words, not just leaving that person or saying, "Now you are on your own." But realizing that wherever there's a need for support, you would be there. Giving that kind of a support. And I'm sure that's what came to my mind most.

Finally, Mosola responded to my posing of Sleeter's (2001a) question, "Do teachers feel that this teacher education course had any long-term influence on their subsequent teaching practices?" in the following way:

Actually, certainly, yes, the course has influenced my teaching. In fact, I've just been promoted to head of the department. And also, with the teachers themselves, I have initiated a history teachers' forum at my school. Our basis was to have an understanding of the way in which our students write . . . and problems that [the teachers] are encountering when they are actually writing with their students. We wanted to better understand that students are actually writing in the second language. And as a result, the students are naturally feeling that they are not capable or adequate. That was basically our concern. Since taking what we learned in our course, I have been trying to find ways in which we can engage the department of education in ensuring that Xhosa, in particular, and all these other African languages, become part of the writing of the exams. You see, there hasn't been that much that has been written in Xhosa. So we are actually moving forward with this initiative. We want the students to have the form of the history exam paper in Xhosa as well. And for me, one of the reasons this is critically important is that students are actually being encouraged to write in their own languages.

So you see, I am also putting my plans into action with my students. We talked about this plan 3 years ago when I was in your course, and I'm moving forward with it. I decided that now we need to have a group of students themselves, right, who are actually engaging themselves particularly in the writing. In writing stories, in writing history themselves . . . I sit with the students, I actually identify with the students. And we have formed a community. And that community we decided to call ourselves thereafter "A History Club." As I've said that our students have a problem in that when they come to their exam at the end of the year, they struggle because they must write in a language that is not their own. So if we want to make a change, we must draw in those students, those people who are directly affected. . . . Then once again, this is what will have some power. I'm not talking of subtractive bilingualism, I'm talking about additive bilingualism. So in other words, you are not learning one language at the expense of the other, but then you let them both move forward in parallel. We understand that for one to be able to understand their second language, one must have the strength base of the mother tongue. We discussed this in our class. That's encouraging us to move in a direction that will end up making us much stronger. So you see, I care most about my students in the classroom, and I love to see them grappling with issues by themselves, and therefore I think I sometimes use the theories that I actually got from your class.

Niko responded to the same question in the following way:

Yes, the course has influenced me. You see, when I received the call that you were coming, I had come from a meeting which was quite a heated meeting, and it made me . . . you know, I was depressed and I was feeling bad. And then your call came through, and I said, well, here's something worth continuing for. You know, at least there's somebody there who has the right idea about education. So forget about this bunch of people here. So you see it has influenced me to give me a more positive outlook and to give me the hope of change. It has helped me to have a vision for what the larger goal is that I want to accomplish even though small-minded people make it difficult on a day-to-day basis.

It is important to note that several themes from the course were voiced by most of the teachers. These themes included the course's emphasis on a Vygotskian (1962, 1978, 1981) style of teaching that provided scaffolding support for learning, incorporating the students' lived experiences and linguistic resources in the curriculum, and encouraging the eventual independence of the learner. Many teachers also noted the idea of giving voice to the voiceless as a concept that stood out as memorable for them. It is important to point out these teachers' positive reaction to being exposed to theory in the course, since some teacher education programs shy away from introducing theory to the teachers because they fear the teachers will not appreciate its value.

THE TEACHERS' VOICES AS EVIDENCE OF CHANGE AND THE DEVELOPMENT OF EFFICACY

After triangulating the oral and written data collected from the teachers with the follow-up classroom observations and interviews, I learned that it was the teachers' voices that provided the most powerful evidence of the ideological and pedagogical changes that were taking place in their lives. After going through the four stages of the model depicted in Figure 4.1, after engaging with theory in conjunction with using writing as a pedagogical tool that facilitated reflection, introspection, and critique, and after involvement with teacher research projects that required teachers to engage with diverse student populations in thoughtful and reflective ways, the teachers in my study were able to offer some powerful suggestions about how we should restructure teacher education programs to successfully motivate teachers to become interested in effectively teaching diverse students.

These teachers have developed voices of their own concerning recommendations to policy makers and administrators for improving teacher education programs. For example, Monica noted that the existing educational system worked in many ways for many students, but not for most students who are particularly poor, Black, marginalized, and underachieving. One of Monica's most insightful comments revolved around the revelation that ultimately it is the classroom teacher who has the greatest impact on student learning. She saw the need for teachers to be aware of individual students' backgrounds and their cultures. She also stated, "It becomes apparent that educators are increasingly being challenged to do more, do it better, and do it for larger classes of students." She spoke of her own plans to use computers as one way to deal with this challenge because interactive computers would allow her students to start at their own level and proceed at their own speed. But her own voice comes through most strongly as she concludes that it is "the individual teacher who has the greatest power and who needs the support to make this happen for every student, regardless of their race, class, linguistic background, or socioeconomic level."

Nomha, by contrast, voiced frustration, because she felt that students should be allowed to write in their mother tongue, but found that schools do not encourage this—"even though South Africa is supposed to be a multilingual country where the constitution [names] 11 different languages." According to Nomha, teachers are complaining because the students cannot express themselves in English. "And you know what the principal says? He says that English teachers should not use [their] mother tongue, because we will cripple their English development by doing that." However, we are saying, "but how are they going to learn English without . . . using some of their mother tongue? How can they express some of their most deeply felt ideas without using some of their mother tongue?" Nomha was pleased to report that through her advocacy and the advocacy of teachers like her, the principal has moved a little bit more toward agreeing with the teachers' opinion—that students need to be able to use both.

Nomha also noted that teachers needed continuous, ongoing professional development and training and must have access to computers, "so that what I do here in South Africa, I will be able to compare that with what educators are doing somewhere else. . . . So that way, I can get the information and knowledge from other people and improve my own learning. I want more information, more knowledge."

For Irene, "The policy makers and administrators need to know that our teachers at the moment in South Africa are very depressed." Irene recommended that every teacher be trained to do multigrade teaching in student-centered classrooms where teachers can admit that they do not have all the answers. She felt that their inability to do this is a matter of being able to hand over part of their power base in the classroom. "Policy makers and administrators need to deal with this issue, and they need to structure teacher education programs so that new teachers get to deal with these issues about language and diversity before entering the schools."

Finally, Irene recommends that parents have the freedom to come in and out of our classrooms, so they may get involved in their children's education.

Mieko noted that many teachers were very concerned about the current stresses of test-driven curriculum. "Some teachers are losing their dedication, it just isn't there any longer." She noted that there's always changes coming about—one demand here, another there—making teachers feel unstable and insecure. They do not know where they are because "the moment you're about to implement something new, another external demand comes along. So it is all the time, these changes which make for no stability. And this is not good." Mieko added:

> I would say for the teacher who is not fully qualified, not fully credentialed, particularly in poor schools, the school district should set money aside to help those who have the potential to become good teachers . . . because that teacher is just going along and feeling "I'm almost there." But the teacher is not fully developed, not fully trained to do what they're supposed to do. The problem is that there's never adequate funds. So that the teacher stays in the same old rut all the time. And it isn't the fault of that teacher at that time. . . . The funding should come from the administration. Because those teachers don't earn enough money to pay for continuing courses. But their qualifications need to be upgraded.

Gafumbe noted that we need to admit that we live in a multilingual society:

> For example, I live in the Western Cape where the primary language is Xhosa for our school. Now I have suggested to people that we need to look at three languages when we think about the medium of instruction for our students. I'm aware that some people think that children are too young to learn three languages, but by the time our kids reach Grade 6, they've learned basic Xhosa and they are being introduced to English, and then there is Afrikaans. In the United States there is African American English, English, and many Blacks are Spanish speaking as well. So we need as teachers to make people aware that it is not a political ploy to let children come to understand Standard English in the United States and also for us to learn Afrikaans. Because when you understand somebody's language, you understand his culture, you begin to understand his thinking, you begin to understand his fears, his frustrations, his everything. So it is one of the things that I learned from the course the last time we met on multilingualism. That our children should know these languages,

but they cannot get there from the support that they are currently getting. The support needs to be there from the Department of Education because without that support, the children are helpless.

Mosola shared his recommendations this way: "What I think we can actually do is start to ensure that teacher training is not a once-and-for-all thing. It should be a continuous process . . . in which teachers do action research for themselves. This should be one of the things that each teacher should be able to do. They should seriously think again about what it is we do and how we can do it better."

All these teachers have become generative thinkers—reflective, thoughtful, committed action agents with a personal voice that can give direction to our efforts for educational reform. These teachers' experiences in schools with students of color and children of poverty have enabled them to give insightful responses to important questions about education. Their sense of efficacy is displayed in their teaching, and their voices demonstrate how they have become carriers of the torch. I have shared the voices of these U.S. and South African teachers with whom I worked over the past decade because their voices demonstrate their willingness to probe deeply and explore cultural aspects of teaching and learning. Their contemplations on the challenges of working with students from diverse cultural and linguistic groups can help us address the need to restructure teacher education programs. The inscribed reflections of these teachers illustrate their personal journeys as they used writing as a pedagogical tool to promote reflection, introspection, and critique and testify to their active engagement with the theory and carefully designed teaching activities presented in class. As we listen to the voices of these teachers, we are struck by the confidence with which they have come to speak. Their experiences in classrooms with students of color and students from poverty backgrounds allow them to speak with authority on issues of diversity and to share their words of advice. Such information can provide insights that help others to be more effective as teachers, teacher educators, administrators, and policy makers capable of connecting with students from diverse backgrounds in meaningful ways. Through these teachers' texts, I shared the developmental journeys taken by actual teachers on the road to becoming carriers of the torch.

This is but a small sample of the insightful recommendations offered by the dynamic teachers who participated in my course. I realize that I was but one of the teacher educators who worked with these teachers and certainly I cannot take credit for where these teachers came from, who they became, or what they were able to accomplish following their engagement with my course. However, I am convinced that the course influenced their ideological becoming, their changing perspectives, and the powerful practices they embraced and enacted in their classrooms. I am inspired by the knowledge that each of them implemented effective teaching practices for working with students from diverse racial, ethnic, and language groups and helped to establish powerful programs in their schools and communities. I am gratified that each of these teachers went on to pursue further studies in the areas of multilingual or multicultural education. I am convinced that the course influenced these teachers' understanding of the role they could play in improving society and transforming the socioeconomic inequalities reflected in the underresourced schools in which they worked.

As I came to the close of my work with these teachers, I recalled the comments made by Gafumbe early in the program and I reflected on the promise I made to him and to the class on our first day together—my promise to share their voices with the larger educational community and to act as a vehicle for making the voices of teachers heard. The sentiments of many teachers who work in schools that serve poor, disenfranchised, and underachieving students can be heard in the final message that Gafumbe asked me to share with policy makers and administrators in teacher education programs:

> Lastly. . . . our [poor, Black, and underresourced] communities don't have any input into how the district is run because many administrators presume that our classrooms are comprised of the people who are going to become society's custodians for those people who are going to come out of the higher-education system. So the education system—those who decide how the programs will be restructured—is either decided by policy makers, professors, or people like them. But the principals and teacher leaders who work with the poor people of the community and who work in the communities where these people come from, they need to have avenues or mechanisms for making suggestions to those in power because now we have some real problems with teachers who don't perform, people who don't care about what happens in education, people who would go [into teaching] just because they want to get the money. But there must be some mechanism through which those teachers are held accountable to the community. So I would appreciate it, if you ever have an opportunity to consult with those who decide on the restructuring of the education centers for teacher training, please tell those people that *they* should be the main people who are confronted with these matters in our communities. And please tell them that principals and teacher

leaders should be consulted about solutions to the problems we have in education today.

It is my hope that the voices of these teachers and principals will be heard. Because of the work of activist scholars and members of organizations such as the American Educational Research Association's special interest group on social justice and the socially minded members of Division K on teacher education—members who come from mainstream as well as nonmainstream backgrounds—I am hopeful that the voices of teachers are being heard, that teachers are teaching for social justice, and that the voices of these teachers are making an impact on educational reform movements and efforts for social change.

In response to rapid changes in school demographics, Sleeter (2001a) posed a challenge to teacher education programs, asserting that we need to focus on research that investigates what happens in preservice programs that significantly develops their teaching of students from diverse racial, ethnic, and language groups (pp. 219–220). The research that I have reported on in this book addresses that challenge. I report on the results of a teacher education course designed to encourage critical and generative thinking on the part of teachers and document the changing discourses of teachers in the course and the behavioral changes that followed their changing ideologies and perspectives on diversity. Perhaps even more important, this book presents a cross-national study, involving U.S. and South African teachers, that responds to Sleeter's plea for research focusing on teachers' classroom performance in schools in which students of color and students from poverty backgrounds are clustered, to show what happens in the teacher education programs that significantly develop their teaching. Along with other scholars who are preparing teachers to teach for social justice, this research demonstrates how teacher education programs can foster informed, positive attitudes about diversity among teachers. It also contributes to our understanding of the processes of teacher change, how we can use writing as a pedagogical tool to motivate and facilitate teachers' ideological becoming, and how we can use discourse analysis as a tool for documenting that change. I am hopeful that this work will stimulate conversations that can effect change for the most disenfranchised members of our global society. I have no doubt that this work and the work of other thoughtful, committed people can change the world. Indeed, as Margaret Meade has noted, it is the only thing that ever has.

References

Abdullah, S., Kamberelis, G., & McGinley, W. (1992). Literacy, identity, and resistance within the African-American slave community and some reflections for new forms of literacy pedagogy. In C. K. Kinzer & D. J. Leu (Eds.), *Literacy research, theory, and practice: Views from many perspectives* (pp. 379–391). Chicago: National Reading Conference, Inc.

Anderson, J. D. (1988). *The education of Blacks in the South, 1860–1935.* Chapel Hill, NC: University of North Carolina Press.

Anyon, J. (1981). Social class and school knowledge. *Curriculum Inquiry, 11*(1), 3–42.

Armour-Thomas, E., Clay, C., Domanico, R., Bruno, K., & Allen, B. (1989). *An outlier study of elementary and middle schools in New York City: Final report.* New York: New York City Board of Education.

Ashton, P. T., &Webb, R. B. (1986). *Making a difference: Teachers' sense of efficacy and student achievement.* New York: Longman.

Atwell, N. (1993). Foreword. In L. Patterson, C. M. Santa, K. G. Short, & K. Smith (Eds.), *Teachers as researchers: Reflections and action* (pp. vii–x). Newark, DE: International Reading Association.

Au, K. (1994). An expanded definition of literacy. In K. Au, *Literacy instruction in multicultural settings* (pp. 20–34). New York: Harcourt Brace.

Bakhtin, M. M. (1981). *The dialogic imagination.* Austin: University of Texas Press.

Bakhtin, M. (1986). *Speech genres and other late essays.* (C. Emerson & M. Holquist, Eds.; V. W. McGee, Trans.). Austin: University of Texas Press.

Ball, A. F. (1992). Cultural preference and the expository writing of African-American adolescents. *Written Communication, 9*(4), 501–532.

Ball, A. F. (1995a). Community-based learning in urban settings as a model for educational reform. *Applied Behavioral Science Review, 3*(2), 127–146.

Ball, A. F. (1995b). Text design patterns in the writing of urban African-American students: Teaching to the strengths of students in multicultural settings. *Urban Education, 30*(3), 253–289.

Ball, A. F. (1998a). Evaluating the writing of culturally and linguistically diverse students: The case of the African American Vernacular English speaker. In C. R. Cooper & L. Odell (Eds.), *Evaluating writing: The role of teachers' knowledge about text, learning, and culture* (pp. 225–248). Urbana, IL: National Council of Teachers of English Press.

Ball, A. F. (1998b). The value of recounting narratives: Memorable learning experiences in the lives of inner-city students and teachers. *Journal of Narrative Inquiry, 8*(1), 1–30.

Ball, A. F. (1999). Preservice teachers' perspectives on literacy and its use in urban schools: A Vygotskian perspective on internal activity and teacher change. In C. Lee & P. Smagorinsky (Eds.), *Vygotskian perspectives on literacy research: Constructing meaning through collaborative inquiry* (pp. 314–359). Cambridge, UK: Cambridge University Press.

Ball, A. F. (2000). Empowering pedagogies that enhance the learning of multicultural students. *Teachers College Record, 102*(6), 1006–1034.

Ball, A. F. (2002). Three decades of research on classroom life: Illuminating the classroom communicative lives of America's at-risk students. *Review of Research in Education.* New York: AERA.

Ball, A. F. (2003). US and South African teachers' developing perspectives on language and literacy: Changing domestic and international roles of linguistic gatekeepers. In S. Makoni, G. Smitherman, A. F. Ball, & A. K. Spears (Eds.), *Black linguistics: Language, society, and politics in Africa and the Americas.* London, UK: Routledge Press.

Ball, A. F., & Farr, M. (2003). Dialects, culture, and teaching the English language arts. In J. Flood, J. M. Jensen, D. Lapp, & J. R. Squire (Eds.), *Handbook of research on teaching the English language arts.* New York: Macmillan.

Ball, A. F., & Freedman, S. W. (Eds.). (2004). *Bakhtinian perspectives on language, literacy, and learning.* Cambridge, UK: Cambridge University Press.

Ball, A. F., & Lardner, T. (1997). Dispositions toward literacy: Constructs of teacher knowledge and the Ann Arbor Black English case. *College Composition and Communication, 48*(4), 469–485.

Ball, A. F., & Lardner, T. (2005). *African American literacies unleashed: Vernacular English and the composition classroom.* Carbondale, IL: Southern Illinois University Press.

Bandura, A. (1977). Self-efficacy: Toward a unifying theory of behavioral change. *Psychological Review, 84,* 191–215.

Bandura, A. (1986). *Social foundations of thought and action: A social cognitive theory.* Englewood Cliffs, NJ: Prentice Hall.

Bandura, A. (1997). *Self-efficacy: The exercise of control.* New York: W. H. Freeman.

Banks, J. A. (1991). Multicultural literacy and curriculum reform. *Educational Horizons, 69,* 135–140.

Banks, J. A. (Ed.). (1996). *Multicultural education, transformative knowledge, and action: Historical and contemporary perspectives.* New York: Teachers College Press.

Berman, P., McLaughlin, M., Bass, G., Pauly, E., & Zellman, G. (1977). *Federal programs supporting educational change: Vol. VII. Factors affecting implementation and continuation.* Santa Monica, CA: Rand Corporation.

Bhola, H. S. (1994, Oct. 26–28). *Education for reconstruction and development in post-apartheid South Africa: A policy discourse.* Paper commissioned by UNESCO, Paris, for the South African International Donors Conference on Human Resource Development in the Reconstruction and Development Programme, Cape Town, South Africa.

Britton, J. (1975). *The development of writing abilities.* London: Macmillan.

Brown, L. (Ed.). (1987). *A guide to reading narratives or moral conflict and choice for self and moral voice.* Cambridge: Harvard University GEHD Study Center.

Brozo, W. G. (1990). Hiding out in secondary classrooms: Coping strategies of unsuccessful readers. *Journal of Reading, 33,* 324–328.

Bruner, J. S. (1985). Narrative and paradigmatic modes of thought. In E. Eisner (Ed.), *Learning and teaching the ways of knowing* (pp. 97–115). Chicago: National Society for the Study of Education.

Bruner, J. S. (1986). *Actual minds, possible worlds.* Cambridge: Harvard University Press.

Bruner, J. S. (1990). *Acts of meaning.* Cambridge, MA: Harvard University Press.

Bruner, J. S. (1994). Life as narrative. In A. H. Dyson and C. Genishi (Eds.), *The need for story: Cultural diversity in classroom and community.* Urbana, IL: National Council of Teachers of English.

Burnaford, G., Fisher, J., & Hobson, D. (1996). *Teachers doing research: Practical possibilities.* Mahwah, NJ: Lawrence Erlbaum Associates.

California State Department of Education. (2000). [California basic educational data system, public school summary statistics]. Retrieved Aug. 1, 2000, from http://www.cde.ca.gov/ds/

Carnegie Council on Adolescent Development. (1989). *Turning point: Preparing American youth for the 21st century.* New York: Carnegie Corporation.

Carrim, N., & Soudien, C. (1999). Critical anti-racism in South Africa. In S. May (Ed.), *Critical multiculturalism: Multicultural and anti-racist education.* London: Falmer Press.

Cazden, C. (1988). Environmental assistance revisited: Variation and functional equivalence. In F. S. Kessel (Ed.), *The development of language and language researchers: Essays in honor of Roger Brown* (pp. 281–297). Hillsdale, NJ: Lawrence Erlbaum Associates.

Cleage, A. (1968). *The Black Messiah.* New York: Sheed & Ward.

Code, L. (1991). *What can she know? Feminist theory and the construction of knowledge.* Ithaca, New York: Cornell University Press.

Cohen, D. (1990). A revolution in one classroom: The case of Mrs. Oublier. *Educational Evaluation and Policy Analysis, 12*(3), 311–329.

Connelly, F. M., & Clandinin, D. J. (1985a). Personal practical knowledge and the modes of knowing: Relevance for teaching and learning. In E. Eisner (Ed.), *Learning and teaching the ways of knowing* (pp. 174–198). Chicago: National Society for the Study of Education.

Connelly, F. M., & Clandinin, D. J. (1985b). *Teachers as curriculum planners: Narratives of experience.* New York: Teachers College Press.

Connelly, F. M., & Clandinin, D. J. (1990). Stories of experience and narrative inquiry. *Educational Researcher, 19*(5), 2–14.

C2005 Review Committee. (2000). *Curriculum 2005.* Pretoria, South Africa: Department of Education.

Cuban, L. (1984). *How teachers taught.* New York: Longman.

Cuban, L. (1986). *Teachers and machines.* New York: Teachers College Press.

Cummins, J. (1994). Knowledge, power, and identity in teaching English as a second language. In F. Genesee (Ed.), *Educating second language children: The whole child, the whole curriculum, the whole community* (pp. 33–58). New York: Cambridge University Press.

Darling-Hammond, L. (1986). A proposal for evaluation in the teaching profession. *Elementary School Journal, 86,* 531–551.

Darling-Hammond, L. (1990). Teacher quality and equality. In J. I. Goodlad & P. Keating (Eds.), *Access to knowledge: An agenda for our nation's schools* (pp. 237–258). New York: College Entrance Examination Board.

Darling-Hammond, L. (1992). Teaching and knowledge: Policy issues posed by alternate certification for teachers. *Peabody Journal of Education, 67*(3), 123–154.

Darling-Hammond, L. (1995). Inequality and access to knowledge. In J. Banks & C. Banks (Eds.), *Handbook of research on multicultural education.* New York: Macmillan.

Darling-Hammond, L. (1996). The right to learn and the advancement of teaching: Research, policy, and practice for democratic education. *Educational Researcher, 25*(6), 5–17.

Darling-Hammond, L. (1998). Teachers and teaching: Testing policy hypotheses from a national commission report. *Educational Researcher, 27*(10), 5–15.

Davis, R. (1984). Charles T. Loram and the American model for African education in South Africa. In P. Kallaway (Ed.), *Apartheid and education: The education of Black South Africans.* Johannesburg: Ravan Press.

Delpit, L. (1988). The silenced dialogue: Power and pedagogy in educating other people's children. *Harvard Educational Review, 58*(3), 280–298.

Delpit, L. (1992). Acquisition of literacy discourse: Bowing before the master? *Theory into Practice, 31,* 296–302.

Dewey, J. (1934). *Art as experience.* New York: G. P. Putnam's Sons.

Dewey, J. (1938). *Experience and education.* New York: Collier Books.

Dillard, C. B. (1995). Engaging pedagogy: Writing and reflecting in multicultural teacher education. *Teaching Education, 8*(1), 13–21.

Dreeben, R. (1987). Closing the divide: What teachers and administrators can do to help Black students reach their reading potential. *American Educator, 11*(4), 28–35.

Dyson, A. H., & Genishi, C. (Eds.). (1994). *The need for story: Cultural diversity in classroom and community.* Urbana: National Council of Teachers of English.

Emig, J. (1977). Writing as a mode of thinking. *College Composition and Communication, 28*(2), 122–28.

Faust, D. G. (1980). Culture, conflict and community: The meaning of power on an antebellum plantation. In P. Finkelman (Ed.), *The culture and community of slavery* (pp. 83–97). New York: Garland.

Ferguson, R. F. (1991). Paring for public education: New evidence on how and why money matters. *Harvard Journal on Legislation, 28*(2), 465–498.

First to worst. (2003). In J. Merrow (Executive Producer), *The Merrow Report.* Washington, DC: PBS.

Foster, D., & Russell, D. (2002). *Writing and learning in cross-national perspec-*

tive: Transitions from secondary to higher education. Urbana, IL: National Council of Teachers of English/Lawrence Erlbaum.

Fox, S. L. (1992). *Memories of play, dreams of success: Literacy autobiographies of 101 students.* ERIC Document No. ED 348681.

Franklin, J. H., & Moss, A. A. (2000). *From slavery to freedom: A history of African Americans* (8th ed.). New York: A. A. Knopf.

Fredrickson, G. M. (1995). *Black liberation: A comparative history of Black ideologies in the United States and South Africa.* New York: Oxford University Press.

Fredrickson, G. M. (1997). *The comparative imagination: On the history of racism, nationalism, and social movements.* Berkeley: University of California Press.

Fredrickson, G. M. (2004). *Not just black and white: Historical and contemporary perspectives on immigration, race, and ethnicity in the United States.* New York: Russell Sage Foundation.

Freedman, S. W. (1994). *Exchanging writing, exchanging cultures: Lessons in school reform from the United States and Great Britain.* Cambridge, MA: Harvard University Press.

Freeman, D. (1992). To make the tacit explicit: Teacher education, emerging discourse, and conceptions of teaching. *Teaching and Teacher Education, 7,* 439–454.

Freeman, D. (1996). "'To take them at their word': Language data in the study of teachers' knowledge." *Harvard Educational Review, 66*(4), 732–761.

Freire, P. (1970). *Pedagogy of the oppressed.* New York: Continuum.

Gadamer, H. G. (1976). *Philosophical hermeneutics.* Berkeley: University of California Press.

Gee, J. P. (1989). What is literacy? *Journal of Education, 171,* 18–25.

Gee, J. P. (1991). A linguistic approach to narrative. *Journal of Narrative and Life History, 1*(1), 15–39.

Gere, A. (1989). *Roots in the sawdust.* Urbana, IL: National Council of Teachers of English.

Gibson, S., & Dembo, M. (1984). Teacher efficacy: A construct validation. *Journal of Educational Psychology, 76*(4), 569–582.

Giroux, H. A. (1988). *Teachers as intellectuals: Toward a critical pedagogy of learning.* New York: Bergin & Garvey.

Gollnick, D. M. (1995). National and state initiatives for multicultural education. In J. A. Banks & C. A. M. Banks (Eds.), *Handbook of research on multicultural education* (pp. 44–64). New York: Macmillan.

Gomez, M. L. (1993). Prospective teachers' perspectives on teaching diverse children: A review with implications for teacher education and practice. *Journal of Negro Education, 62*(4), 459–474.

Goodenow, R. K., & White, A. O. (Eds.). (1981). *Education and the rise of the new South.* Boston: G. K. Hall.

Grant, C. A., & Secada, W. G. (1990). Preparing teachers for diversity. In W. R. Houston (Ed.), *Handbook of research on teacher education* (pp. 403–422). New York: Macmillan.

Guskey, T. (1988). Teacher self-efficacy, self-concept, and attitudes toward the implementation of instructional innovation. *Teacher and Teacher Education*, 4(1), 63–69.

Hannaway, J. (1990). *Breaking the cycle: Instructional efficacy and teachers of at-risk students*. Center for Research on the Context of Secondary School Teaching, Stanford University.

Harding, S. (1991). *Whose science? Whose knowledge? Thinking from women's lives*. Ithaca, NY: Cornell University Press.

Hardy, B. (1977). Narrative as a primary act of mind. In M. Meek, A. Warlow, & G. Barton (Eds.), *The cool web: The patterns of children's reading* (pp. 12–23). New York: Atheneum.

Harste, J. C., Leland, C., Schmidt, K., Vasquez, V., & Ociepka, A. (2004). Practice makes practice, or does it? The relationship between theory and practice in teacher education. *Reading Online*, 7. http://www.readingonline.org/articles/art_index.asp?HREF=/articles/harste.

Hartshorne, K. (1992). *Crisis and challenge: Black education, 1910–1990*. Cape Town: Oxford University Press.

Henning, E. (2000). Walking with "barefoot" teachers: an ethnographically fashioned casebook. *Teaching and Teacher Education*, 16(1), 3–20.

hooks, b., & West, C. (1991). *Breaking bread: Insurgent Black intellectual life*. Boston: South End Press.

Howie, S. J. (2003). Conditions of schooling in South Africa and the effects on mathematics achievement. *Studies in Educational Evaluation*, 29, 227–241.

Hudelson, S. (1994). Literacy development of second language children. In F. Genesee (Ed.), *Educating second language children: The whole child, the whole curriculum, the whole community* (pp. 129–158). New York: Cambridge University Press.

Hyslop, J. (1988). School student movements and state education policy: 1972–87. In W. Cobbett & R. Coben (Eds.), *Popular struggles in South Africa* (pp. 183–209). Trenton, NJ: Africa World Press.

Hyslop, J. (1900). Teacher resistance in African education from the 1980s. In M. Nkomo (Ed.), *Pedagogy of domination* (pp. 93–119). Trenton, NJ: Africa World Press.

Irvine, J. (2003). *Educating Teachers for diversity: Seeing with a cultural eye*. New York: Teachers College Press.

Jansen, J. (1990). Curriculum as a political phenomenon: Historical reflections on Black South African education. *Journal of Negro Education* (59)2, 195–206.

Jansen, J. (2001). Explaining non-change in education reform after apartheid: Political symbolism and the problem of policy implementation. In J. Jansen & Y. Sayed (Eds.), *Implementing education policies: The South African experience* (pp. 271–292). Cape Town, South Africa: University of Cape Town Press.

Kallaway, P. (Ed.) (1984). *Apartheid and education*. Johannesburg: Ravan Press.

Kemmis, S. (1988). Action research. In J. Keeves (Ed.), *Educational research, methodology, and measurement*. Oxford: Pergamon Press.

King, J. E., & Ladson-Billings, G. (1990). The teacher education challenge in elite university settings: Developing critical perspectives for teaching in a democratic and multicultural society. *European Journal of Intercultural Studies*, 1(2), 15–30.

King, J. E., & Mitchell, C. A. (1990). *Black mothers to sons: Juxtaposing African American literature with social practice*. New York: Lang.

Knowles, L. L., & Prewitt, K. (1969). *Institutional racism in America*. Englewood Cliffs, NJ: Prentice Hall.

Kozol, J. (1992). *Savage inequalities: Children in America's schools*. New York: Harper.

Labov, W. (1972). The transformation of experience in narrative syntax. In W. Labov (Ed.), *Language in the inner city: Studies in the black vernacular* (pp. 354–399). Philadelphia: University of Pennsylvania Press.

Labov, W. (1982). Speech actions and reactions in personal narrative. In D. Tannen (Ed.), *Analyzing discourse: Text and talk*. Washington, DC: Georgetown University Press.

Lampert, M. (1988). *Teachers' thinking about students' thinking about geometry: The effects of new teaching tools*. Cambridge: Educational Technology Center.

Langer, J., & Applebee, A. (1987). *How writing shapes thinking*. Urbana, IL: NCTE.

Lee, C. D. (1995). Signifying as a scaffold for literary interpretation. *Journal of Black Psychology*, 21(4), 357–381.

Lee, C. D. (2000). Signifying in the zone of proximal development. In C. D. Lee & P. Smagorinsky (Eds.), *Vygotskian perspectives on literacy research: Constructing meaning through collabative inquiry* (pp. 191–225). Cambridge, UK: Cambridge University Press.

Lee, C. D. (2001). Is October Brown Chinese: A cultural modeling activity system for underachieving students. *American Educational Research Journal*, 38(1), 97–142.

Lee, C. D., & Ball, A. F. (2005). All that glitters ain't gold: CHAT as a design and analytical tool in literacy research. In R. Beach, J. Green, M. Kamil, & T. Shanahan (Eds.), *Multidisciplinary perspectives on literacy research* (2nd ed., pp. 101–132). Cresskill, NJ: Hampton Press.

Leont'ev, A. N. (1981). The problem of activity in psychology. In J. Wertsch (Ed.), *The concept of activity in Soviet psychology*. Armonk/White Plains, NY: Sharpe.

Luria, A. R. (1981). *Language and cognition* (J. V. Wertsch, Ed.). New York: Wiley.

Malarkey, T. W. (1992). *The politics of teacher efficacy and education reform: The case of South Africa*. Unpublished SIDEC master's monograph, Stanford University School of Education.

McDonnell, L. M., Timpane, P. M., & Benjamin, R. (Eds.). (2000). *Rediscovering the democratic purposes of education*. Lawrence: University Press of Kansas.

McElroy-Johnson, B. (1993). Teaching and practice: Giving voice to the voiceless. *Harvard Educational Review*, 63(1), 85–104.

McEwan, H., & Egan, K. (1995). *Narrative in teaching, learning, and research*. New York: Teachers College Press.

Meyer, J. W., & Rowan, B. (1978). Institutionalized organizations: Formal structures as myth and ceremony. *American Journal of Sociology*, 83, 340–363.

Midgely, C., Feldlaufer, H., & Eccles, J. (1989). Change in teacher efficacy and student self- and task-related beliefs in mathematics during the transition to junior high school. *Journal of Educational Psychology, 81*(2), 247–258.

Moodley, K. A., & Adam, H. (2003). Citizenship education and political literacy in South Africa. In J. Banks (Ed.), *Diversity and citizenship education: Global perspectives* (pp. 159–184). San Francisco: Jossey Bass.

Mncwabe, M. P. (1989). *Teacher neutrality and education in crisis: The Black teacher's dilemma in South Africa.* Braamfontein: Skotaville Educational Division.

Mncwabe, M. P. (1990). *Separate and equal education: South Africa's education at the crossroads.* Durban: Butterworths.

Mncwabe, M. P. (1993). *Post-apartheid education: Towards non-racial, unitary, and democratic socialization in the new South Africa.* Lanham: University Press of America.

National Association for Multicultural Education (NAME). (2003). *Definition.* Retrieved Feb. 1, 2003, from http://www.nameorg.org/resolutions/definition.html

National Center for Education Statistics. (1994). *Characteristics of the 100 largest public elementary and secondary school districts in the United States: 1991–1992.* Washington, DC: Author.

National Center for Education Statistics. (1999–2000). *School and staffing survey.* Washington, DC: U.S. Department of Education.

National Commission on Teaching and America's Future. (1996). *What matters most: Teaching for America's future.* New York: Author.

National Data Resources Center (NDRC). (1992). *Schools and staffing survey, 1990–1991.* Unpublished tabulations of data.

National Education Association. (1997). *America's teachers.* Retrieved Aug. 15, 1997, from http://www.nea.org/

Nkomo, M. O. (1984). *Student culture and activism in Black South African universities: The roots of resistance.* Westport, CT : Greenwood Press.

Nkomo, M. O. (1990). *Pedagogy of domination: Toward a democratic education in South Africa.* Trenton, NJ: Africa World Press.

Noguera, P. A. (1995). Preventing and producing violence: A critical analysis of responses to school violence. *Harvard Educational Review, 65*(2), 190–212.

Novicki, M. A. (1985, January 7–10). *Toward a new Africa policy: Conference report, the African-American Conference.* Libreville, Gabon.

Oakes, J. (1985). *Keeping track: How schools structure inequality.* New Haven, CT: Yale University Press.

Oakes, J. (1990). *Multiplying inequalities: The effects of race, social class, and tracking on opportunities to learn mathematics and science.* Santa Monica, CA: RAND Corporation.

Omond, R. (1986). *The apartheid handbook* (2nd ed.). New York: Viking Penguin.

Orfield, G., Bachmeier, M. D., James, D. R., & Eitle, T. (1997). *Deepening segregation in American public schools.* Cambridge, MA: Harvard University Project of School Desegregation.

Orfield, G., & Reardon, S. F. (1993). *Race, poverty, and inequality.* Cambridge, MA: Harvard University Project of School Desegregation.

Pang, V. O., & Sablan, V. (1995). *Teacher efficacy: Do teachers believe they can be effective with African American students?* Paper presented at the annual meeting of the American Educational Research Association, San Francisco.

Popkewitz, T. S. (1976). *Teacher education as a process of socialization: The social distribution of knowledge* (ERIC Document No. ED 129714). Paper presented at the American Education Research Association annual convention, San Francisco.

Quality Education for Minority Project. (1990). *Education that works: An action plan for the education of minorities.* Cambridge: Massachusetts Institute of Technology.

Richardson, V. (Ed.). (1994). *Teacher change and the staff development process: A case in reading instruction.* New York: Teachers College Press.

Rosenholtz, S. J. (1986). Career ladders and merit pay: Capricious fads or fundamental reforms? *Elementary School Journal, 86*(4), 513–529.

Samuel, J. (1992). The ANC view. In R. McGregor & A. McGregor (Eds.), *McGregor's Education Alternatives* (pp. 107–130). Kenwyn, South Africa: Juta.

Schultz, K. (2003). *Listening: A framework for teaching across differences.* New York: Teachers College Press.

Schwab, J. J. (1973). The practical, 3: Translation into curriculum. *School Review, 81*(4), 501–522.

Schwab, J. J. (1977). Structure of the discipline: Meanings and significances. In A. A. Bellack & H. M. Kliebard (Eds.), *Curriculum and evaluation* (pp. 189–207). Berkeley, CA: McCutchan.

Schwab, J. J. (1983). The practical, 4: Something for curriculum professors to do. *Curriculum Inquiry, 13*(3), 239–256.

Sewage problems, chemicals, lead poisoning, contamination. (1989, April 2). St. Louis Post-Dispatch, p. 8.

Sleeter, C. E. (2001a). Epistemological diversity in research on preservice teacher preparation for historically underserved children. *Review of Research in Education, 25,* 209–250.

Sleeter, C. E. (2001b). Preparing teachers for culturally diverse schools: Research and the overwhelming presence of Whiteness. *Journal of Teacher Education, 52*(2), 94–106.

Soudien, C. (1998). Our school is not Coloured: Struggling with identity at City Central, Cape Town, South Africa. In N. Bak (Ed.), *Going for the gap.* Cape Town: Juta.

Soudien, C. (2004). "Constructing the class": An analysis of the process of "integration" in South African schools. In L. Chisholm (Ed.), *Changing class: Education and social change in post-apartheid South Africa* (pp. 89–114). London: Zed Books.

Stubbs, M. (1983). *Discourse analysis: The sociolinguistic analysis of natural language.* Chicago: University of Chicago Press.

Taylor, D., & Dorsey-Gaines, C. (1988). *Growing up literate: Learning from inner-city families.* Portsmouth, NH: Heinemann.

Tharp, R. G., & Gallimore, R. (1988). *Rousing minds to life: Teaching, learning, and schooling in social context.* New York: Cambridge University Press.

Tschannen-Moran, M., Woolfolk Hoy, A. E., & Hoy, W. K. (1998). Teacher efficacy: Its meaning and measure. *Review of Educational Research, 68*(2), 228.

Tschannen-Moran, M., Woolfolk Hoy, A. E., & Hoy, W. K. (2001). Teacher efficacy: Capturing an elusive construct. *Teaching and Teacher Education, 17,* 783–805.

UNICEF. (2005). *At a glance: South Africa statistics.* Retrieved Oct. 4, 2005, from http://www.unicef.org/infobycountry/southafrica_statistics.html#5

UNESCO Institute for Statistics. (2005). *Country profile.* Retrieved Oct. 4, 2005, from http://www.uis.unesco.org/countryprofiles/html/EN/countryProfile_en .aspx?code=7100.htm

Vygotsky, L. S. (1962). *Thought and language.* (E. Hanfmann and G. Vakar, Trans.). Cambridge: MIT Press.

Vygotsky, L. S. (1978). *Mind in society: The development of higher psychological processes.* (M. Cole, V. John-Steiner, S. Scribner, and E. Souberman, Eds.). Cambridge, MA: Harvard University Press.

Vygotsky, L. S. (1981). The genesis of higher mental functions. In J. Wertsch (Ed.), *The concept of activity in Soviet psychology.* Armonk/White Plains, NY: Sharpe.

Walker, M. (1991). Action research and teaching for people's education. In E. Unterhalter (Ed.), *Apartheid education and popular struggles.* Atlantic Highlands, NJ: Zed.

Walker, V. S., & Archung, K. N. (2003). The segregated schooling of Blacks in the southern United States and South Africa. *Comparative Education Review, 47*(1), 21–40.

Watkins, W. H. (2001). *The White architects of Black education: Ideology and power in America, 1865–1954.* New York: Teachers College Press.

Webster's third new international dictionary unabridged. (1986). Springfield, MA: Merriam-Webster.

Weisman, E. M., & Garza, S. A. (2002). Preservice teacher attitudes toward diversity: Can one class make a difference? *Equity and Excellence in Education, 35*(1), 28–34.

Wertsch, J. (Ed.). (1985). *Culture, communication, and cognition: Vygotskian Perspectives.* Cambridge, UK: Cambridge University Press.

Wertsch, J. (1991). *Voices of the mind: A sociocultural approach to mediated action.* Cambridge, MA: Harvard University Press.

Wertsch, J. V., & Stone, C. A. (1985). The concept of internalization in Vygotsky's account of the genesis of higher mental functions. In J. V. Wertsch (Ed.), *Culture, communication, and cognition: Vygotskian Perspectives* (pp. 162–182). Cambridge, UK: Cambridge University Press.

Wittgenstein, L. (1969). *On certainty* (G. E. M. Anscombe & G. E. von Wright, Eds.; D. Paul & G. E. M. Anscombe, Trans.). New York: Harper, 1969.

Woodson, C. G. (1977). *The mis-education of the Negro.* New York: AMS Press.

Zinchenko, A. (1981). Involuntary memory and the goal-directed nature of activity. In J. V. Wertsch (Ed. and Trans.), *The concept of activity in Soviet psychology* (pp. 300–340). White Plains, NY: M. E. Sharpe. (Original work published 1962)

Index

About the Author

ARNETHA F. BALL is Associate Professor of Education at Stanford University, where she has taught for the past 7 years. Prior to that, she taught at the University of Michigan (1992–1999), where she received an Outstanding Teaching Award in 1998. Her research interests focus on the oral and written literacies of culturally and linguistically diverse populations in formal and informal learning environments in the United States and South Africa. In particular, she focuses on research in writing and writing instruction and the preparation of teachers to work effectively with poor, marginalized, and underachieving students. She combines sociocultural and linguistic theory to investigate the discourse practices of students in classrooms and community-based organizations across national boundaries and provide insights on teacher professional development and the successful pedagogies of teachers who work effectively with students from diverse racial, ethnic, and linguistic groups. This research is applicable to the teaching and learning of a wide range of students and has broad educational implications. It emphasizes the importance of bridging the gap between research on secondary and college students and the importance of incorporating students' cultural resources into the curriculum. Before entering the professorate, Dr. Ball had taught preschool, elementary, and secondary students for more than 25 years and was the founder and Executive Director of Children's Creative Workshop, an early education center that specialized in providing premiere educational experiences for students from diverse backgrounds. Dr. Ball has served as an Academic Specialist for the United States Information Services Program in South Africa, co-taught courses on multiliteracies and English methodologies in the teacher education program at Johannesburg College of Education, and taught in the Further Diploma in Education program at the University of Cape Town. She has served on many boards and committees in her field and has published widely, with numerous book chapters and articles in journals, including *Linguistics and Education*, *Applied Behavioral Science Review*, *Teaching and Teacher Education*, and *Written Communication*. Dr. Ball is a co-editor of two recently published books, *Black Linguistics*, with Dr. Sinfree Makoni, Dr. Geneva Smitherman, and Dr. Arthur Spears, and *Bakhtinian Perspectives on Language, Literacy, and Learning*, with Dr. Sarah Freedman. She is also the co-author of *African American Literacies Unleashed*, with Dr. Ted Lardner. Dr. Ball received the Richard Braddock Award, also with Dr. Ted Lardner, for a *College Composition and Communication*'s outstanding journal article published in 1997.